CAMBRIDGE MUSIC HANDBOOKS

Bruckner: Symphony No. 8

Anton Bruckner's Eighth Symphony (1890), one of the great Romantic symphonies, is a grandly complex masterpiece. Its critical reception has been
fascinatingly contentious. Its music, at once extensive and distilled, directly
confronts the problem of the symphony after Beethoven and after Wagner.
This book explores this many-faceted work from several angles. It documents
the complicated and often misunderstood history of the symphony's composition and revision and offers an accessible guide to its musical design. It demon-
strates, by means of a study of well-known recordings, how performance styles
have evolved in this century. It also revisits the conventional wisdom about the
various versions and editions of the symphony and comes to some provocative
new conclusions.

BENJAMIN KORSTVEDT is Assistant Professor of Music at the University of
St. Thomas, St. Paul, Minnesota. He is currently writing a book on Bruckner
and musical culture in the decades around 1900.

CAMBRIDGE MUSIC HANDBOOKS

GENERAL EDITOR Julian Rushton

Anton Bruckner: Symphony No. 8

Benjamin M. Korstvedt

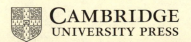
CAMBRIDGE
UNIVERSITY PRESS

PUBLISHED BY THE PRESS SYNDICATE OF THE UNIVERSITY OF CAMBRIDGE
The Pitt Building, Trumpington Street, Cambridge, United Kingdom

CAMBRIDGE UNIVERSITY PRESS
The Edinburgh Building, Cambridge CB2 2RU, UK   http://www.cup.cam.ac.uk
40 West 20th Street, New York NY 10011-4211, USA   http://www.cup.org
10 Stamford Road, Oakleigh, Melbourne 3166, Australia

First published 2000

Printed in the United Kingdom at the University Press, Cambridge

Typeset in Ehrhardt (MT) 10½/13pt, in QuarkXPress™   [SE]

A catalogue record for this book is available from the British Library

Library of Congress cataloguing in publication data
Korstvedt, Benjamin M.
Anton Bruckner, Symphony no. 8 / Benjamin M. Korstvedt.
p.   cm. – (Cambridge music handbooks)
Includes bibliographical references (p.   ) and index.
ISBN 0 521 63226 9 (hardback) – ISBN 0 521 63537 3 (paperback)
1. Bruckner, Anton, 1824–1896.   Symphonies, no. 8, C minor.
I. Title.   II. Series.
ML410.B88K67   2000
784.2′184–dc21   99-31880   CIP

ISBN 0 521 63226 9 hardback
ISBN 0 521 63537 3 paperback

41338194

For Paula and Sam

Contents

Preface and acknowledgments

Scholarly writing about Bruckner typically follows certain well-worn paths; in particular, it tends to grant great emphasis to the notorious editorial problems that attend this composer's works. This book does undoubtedly devote more attention to text-critical concerns than do most others in the Handbook series, partly because the textual history of the Eighth Symphony is complex and important, and partly because modern understanding of it is, as I hope to show, somewhat mistaken. Editorial issues can, if approached with a critical spirit, open out into regions of broader significance, such as hermeneutics, reception history, and performance practice; yet I believe that the "Bruckner Problem" is ordinarily framed too simplistically, and that a reductive concern with textual authenticity has come to loom too large in the imagination of most Brucknerians. For these reasons some parts of this book, notably Chapters 3 and 4, are deliberately unburdened by text-critical concerns.

Books that are apt for teaching advanced courses on late nineteenth-century music are not thick on the ground. I have borne this in mind while writing this volume, and will be gratified if it finds use in the classroom. I have tried to provide enough variety amongst the chapters to offer some small methodological range (from critical analysis and reception history, to textual history, with even a hint of the history of ideas in the chapter on the sublime) for an enterprising teacher to build upon.

I owe great thanks to my wife Paula for her staunch support and help, and for her patience in hearing great gusts of and about the Eighth Symphony. Our son Sam was, like Paula, a constant, glowing beacon of light and love.

Many other people earned my gratitude by offering me assistance of various kinds. Laurence Dreyfus generously shared with me the text of a crucial letter from Levi to Bruckner he had uncovered in Munich.

Morten Solvik, Derek Scott and Juan Cahis gave me copies of then-unpublished articles. Henry Lea and Lionel Tacchini aided me with some knotty problems of translation. Dermot Gault, Gunnar Cohrs, Paul Hawkshaw, and John Phillips helped me with some details about manuscript sources. Amie McEvoy of *The Musical Quarterly* responded with courtesy and promptness to an importune request, as did the Music Division of the Library of Congress. Thomas Christensen and David Aldeborgh lent me copies of rare scores. The conductor Georg Tintner shared with me some perceptive thoughts about the different versions of the symphony. Lani Spahr and Dave Griegel gave me invaluable discographic assistance, as did Mark Kluge. He and William Carragan both read portions of the manuscript and generously shared with me insights and ideas about textual issues and the history of Bruckner performance. I also thank Julian Rushton for his many helpful editorial suggestions, and Penny Souster for suggesting the project to me. Thanks, too, to the Bruckner Gang.

Throughout the course of my work I was thankful to be dealing with a symphony of such superb depth and complex satisfaction.

My final months of work on the book were supported by a Fellowship from the National Endowment for the Humanities, for which I am grateful.

A note on editions and terminology

Four distinct editions of the Eighth Symphony have been published: the first published score (Berlin and Vienna: Haslinger-Schlesinger-Lienau, 1892 [plate number 8288]; later reprinted by Eulenburg, Peters, and Universal Edition), Robert Haas's edition (Leipzig: Musikwissenschaftlicher Verlag, 1939), and Leopold Nowak's critical editions of Bruckner's 1890 and 1887 versions (Vienna: Musikwissenschaftlicher Verlag, 1955 and 1972, respectively).

Nowak's two editions are primary. These scores, which are based closely on Bruckner's manuscript scores of the symphony, are widely accepted by scholars as definitive and are easily available. They are generally identified in this text as simply "the 1887 version" and "the 1890 version." Nowak's edition of the 1890 version is the central source of the Eighth Symphony, and unless otherwise noted, the discussions in this book are based on it.

The edition published in 1939 by Nowak's predecessor, Robert Haas, is not a reasonably faithful representation of either of Bruckner's versions, and is not therefore of primary concern in this study. See Appendix A for a commentary on Haas's edition.

The text of the Eighth Symphony contained in the 1892 edition differs in some ways from the text of Bruckner's manuscript score of the 1890 version. It raises special questions, and is discussed in detail in Chapter 6. It is referred to herein as "the 1892 edition."

Introduction

Meine Achte ist ein Mysterium!
Anton Bruckner[1]

Bruckner's Eighth Symphony, the last he completed, embodies the composer's work, with all of its complexities and contradictions, in its late flowering. This symphony, at once extensive and distilled, has attracted the passionate attention of listeners, musicians, scholars, and critics, yet it remains fascinatingly inscrutable. Bruckner was correct: the Eighth Symphony has proven a mystery. Of all of his symphonies, it poses the most elaborate questions. Musically it stands in complex relationship with the symphonic genre. The grandeur, expressive intensity, and scope of the work directly confront the problem of the symphony after Beethoven and after Wagner, and with its vaguely articulated program it inhabits the crucial space "between absolute and program music."[2] In performance, the symphony has always challenged both interpreters and listeners, and has engendered both exuberant praise and vociferous criticism.

Nowadays to address the Eighth Symphony, or indeed any facet of Bruckner's work, critically means inevitably attending to modern traditions of reception. Our perceptions of Bruckner are mediated by the conceptual residue of preceding generations of interpreters; this is true of any artist, but with Bruckner the situation is particularly acute. Images of Bruckner as a simple genius, an unwitting mystic, a Parsifal-like *naïf* have long shaped attitudes toward him and his music. His music is also shadowed by a long tradition of negative criticism. In the nineteenth century, one important body of opinion decried Bruckner's compositional approach as illogical, incapable of supporting large-scale

1

structures, and thus fundamentally unsuited to the genre of the symphony. The charge continues to sound in this century; American reception of Bruckner in particular still betrays its traces. Bruckner's music largely does not figure in the American musicological canon, and perhaps because of the great influence of Heinrich Schenker, who frankly disdained Bruckner's music, American music theorists have all but ignored Bruckner. The belief that Bruckner is a "lesser composer" is not uncommon in many academic circles.[3] Although the partiality and mistakenness of these notions are increasingly evident, they are so well entrenched in public consciousness that new interpretations remain dependent on them, if only negatively.

Modern understanding of the musical text of the Eighth Symphony is also oddly partial. The compositional history of the symphony was unusually involved and circuitous, and scholars have both elucidated and obscured the genesis and evolution of the work. On the one hand, Leopold Nowak's publication (in 1972) of the initial version of the symphony made available a text of signal importance that had been unpublished for more than eighty years. On the other hand, our understanding of the final version of the symphony has been complicated and indeed clouded by modern editors. The text of the symphony that was published by Bruckner in 1892, and which was the only score known and performed for nearly five decades, has been entirely abandoned as an inauthentic redaction. While this position is not without some basis in fact, it misconstrues the significance of the 1892 edition and obscures an important historical phase of the symphony. Finally, the first modern edition of the symphony, edited by Robert Haas in 1939 and successfully promoted as the first publication of Bruckner's authentic text, is in reality something quite different. Haas's edition, which has found many partisans, does rely in the main on Bruckner's final manuscript text, but it also contains substantial editorial reworking and conflates parts of two distinct versions (see Appendix A). Bruckner's final manuscript text was not published until 1955.

Clearly the Eighth Symphony invites interpretation, both as musical work and as historical text. This volume accepts this invitation by thinking through anew its music, its genesis, its reception, and its various meanings.

1

Placing the Eighth Symphony

In late nineteenth-century Vienna the symphony was fraught with cultural significance; it was widely seen as the musical genre, if not the art form, that most directly could, as Paul Bekker later put it, build a "community of feeling," a process of acute significance in the Habsburg Empire at a time when the old imperial system was increasingly strained by ethnic, nationalist, and democratic impulses.[1] As a result, music became the focus of great cultural and political energy, and aesthetic judgments often encoded cultural politics; in particular, Wagner and the "Music of the Future" excited nationalist, Socialist, racist, and aestheticist sentiments and fueled the energies of segments of society, especially youth, alienated by the liberalism and rationalism of the established social order. Bruckner's symphonies, with their epic grandeur, monumentality, expressive fervor, and harmonic complexity, were widely linked to this Wagnerian ethos and cast as radical counterweights to the concert works of Brahms, who hewed more closely to traditional stylistic canons and, not coincidentally, was solidly entrenched as the composer of the Viennese bourgeois establishment. The critical reception of Bruckner's symphonies makes it quite clear that, intentionally or not, they antagonized segments of the haute bourgeoisie.

It was in this context that the Eighth Symphony received its premiere. The symphony was the sole work in the Vienna Philharmonic subscription concert conducted by Hans Richter on 18 December 1892. Bruckner's music had only rarely appeared on the program of a Philharmonic subscription concert.[2] The Philharmonic was a great bastion of bourgeois traditionalism and its regular patrons were generally ill-disposed – culturally and politically as well as musically – toward Bruckner's music. The Eighth, which was accompanied by a lengthy explanatory program written by Bruckner's young advocate Josef Schalk, did not go down easily with the Philharmonic subscribers, many of whom left after each

3

movement. Eduard Hanslick, the *éminence grise* of the group, ostentatiously left before the Finale, and his departure was greeted by sarcastic applause from Bruckner's supporters. (Bruckner later said that had Hanslick stayed he would only have been "even angrier by the end.")[3] In contrast, the concert generated great interest in other circles – it produced the season's biggest sale of standing room tickets – and the hall held many enthusiasts in addition to the dubious old guard.[4] Brahms attended the concert, as did many prominent supporters of Bruckner, including Hugo Wolf, Johann Strauss, Siegfried Wagner, Crown Princess Stephanie, Archduchess Maria Theresa, and the Bayreuth ideologue Houston Stewart Chamberlain. (The Emperor, to whom the symphony was dedicated, was off on a hunting trip.)

Previous Viennese performances of Bruckner's symphonies had invariably provoked energetic disagreement among competing factions of the musical community. An influential segment of Viennese musical opinion headed by Hanslick and Brahms vigorously opposed Bruckner's claim on the symphonic genre. Bruckner was hailed in other quarters as the herald of a new epoch of the symphony, and as Beethoven's true heir. The premiere of the Eighth Symphony marked a turning point in this conflict. While the concert did not wholly win over Bruckner's antagonists, it did seem to convince them that, if nothing else, Bruckner had finally secured a lasting place as a symphonist. As Theodor Helm saw it, "the artistic triumph Bruckner celebrated on 18 December belongs among the most brilliant of his fame-filled career, because the tumultuous applause came not only from his friends and admirers, but from the entire public."[5] One reviewer even suggested that "a breath of reconciliation wafted . . . over the parties that have battled for years *for* and *against* Bruckner."[6] Even Hanslick's famously negative review of the symphony betrays a hint of placation:

> I found this newest one, as I have found the other Bruckner symphonies, interesting in detail, but strange as a whole, indeed repellent. The peculiarity of this work consists, to put it briefly, of importing Wagner's dramatic style into the symphony . . . In each of the four movements, especially the first and third, some interesting passages, flashes of genius, shine through – if only the rest of it was not there! It is not impossible that the future belongs to this nightmarish hangover style – a future we therefore do not envy![7]

Hanslick had a long, difficult, and personal, relationship with Bruckner. In the early 1870s, when Bruckner was still a relatively minor figure, Hanslick wrote favorably of him as organist and church composer, but in 1874–5 Hanslick staunchly, and ultimately ineffectively, opposed Bruckner's efforts to obtain a position at the University of Vienna (where Hanslick was on the faculty). As Bruckner's prestige and international success as a symphonic composer waxed – and as his Wagnerian affiliations grew clearer – Hanslick's opposition intensified. In the 1880s he wrote a series of openly antagonistic reviews of Viennese performances of Bruckner's symphonies. Soon Hanslick's position became so obvious and the battle-lines so clearly drawn that his criticism became a sort of reverse praise: in 1886 an advertisement for Bruckner's Seventh Symphony included not only the expected plaudits from various critics, but also Hanslick's verdict that the work was "unnaturally presumptuous, diseased and pernicious [*unnatürlich aufgeblasen, krankhaft, und verderblich*]."[8] By these standards, Hanslick's review of the Eighth is not decisively damning. Less than alarm and vituperation, it expresses a rather resigned concession that personal taste aside, Bruckner's star might, for better or worse, be ascendant. Hanslick's protégé Max Kalbeck also admitted stubborn praise: "overall [the symphony] made a surprisingly favorable impression . . . It surpasses Bruckner's earlier works in clarity of arrangement, lucidity of organization, incisiveness of expression, refinement of detail, and logic of thought, but this in no way means that we should accept it as a model of its genre worthy of imitation."[9] Like Hanslick, Kalbeck acknowledged the work's relative merits, but he still suggested that "a third of the expansive score" could well "be thrown overboard" and with his disavowal of the work as a "model," he betrayed a deeper uneasiness over what the work and its success might portend.

Bruckner's partisans saw the work as a culminating achievement, even, as one critic put it, "unreservedly, the crown of music of our time."[10] These enthusiasts judged the work by different standards than did Hanslick and Kalbeck; they were less troubled by the symphony's novelties of form and style, and more impressed by its expressive intensity and compositional boldness. Many also felt that it embodied a sympathetic *Weltanschauung*. A review published in the Catholic paper *Das Vaterland*, which lauded Bruckner for "blazing a path of conviction," explicitly rejected classicizing standards of evaluation and directly took issue with the "main charge" leveled at Bruckner, namely "shortcoming of logic in the structure of his works." "It is not to be denied," wrote the anonymous reviewer, "that Bruckner's fantasy reaches beyond the *established artforms*, that some contrasts strike us as overt, that some repetitions appear superfluous . . . But how do such actions infringe on logic? . . . This is precisely greatness and sublimity in symphonic artworks: the Master does indeed find a framework for the new creation of his fantasy in the basic pattern of the old building, but the fresh springs of his creative powers must not seep away into the ruins of rigid artforms."[11] Josef Stolzing, writing in the *völkisch* journal *Ostdeutsche Rundschau*, explained the significance of the Eighth with words worthy of Bayreuth: "what makes Bruckner so valuable a musician is his unconscious recognition of the true mission of music, namely the direct illustration of the primordial [*urewig*] shaping, destroying, conflicting world-feeling elements [*Welt-Gefühls-Elemente*]."[12] Hugo Wolf wrote simply, "this symphony is the work of a giant and surpasses the other symphonies of the master in intellectual scope, awesomeness, and greatness. Its success was . . . a complete victory of light over darkness."[13] This success was measured at least as much by the relatively conciliatory reactions of Bruckner's old nemeses as by the praise of his partisans.

Changing critical criteria

Over the last century, the critical coordinates by which the Eighth Symphony has been located have shifted and shifted again. For the first decades of its existence, judgments of the symphony were still generally framed by the poles established in Bruckner's Vienna. Laudatory responses unreservedly (and usually airily) praised the spiritual depth and expressive strength of the symphony, often to the edge of hagiolatry: Karl Grunsky wrote that "in the Eighth strife and struggle emerge with primeval force . . . One thinks inevitably of Prometheus or Faust."[14] Negative appraisals carried forward Hanslick's line of criticism and focused on Bruckner's perceived lack of logical coherence and stylistic propriety. Schenker, to take an acute example, found in the Eighth a disturbing mixture of thematic inspiration and compositional failure. The symphony "begins so splendidly, like the beginning of the world," but soon loses its way as Bruckner is betrayed by his inability "to allow two musical thoughts [*Gedanken*] to follow each other properly." Thus he can only "seek vainly to spin a thought by adding up moments of inspiration" and this "will not achieve unity." "The individual tone-words [*Tonworte*] follow one another without necessary connection so that . . . the thought admits no inner need for a middle, a beginning, or even an end."[15] Like Hanslick and Kalbeck, Schenker's severe judgment contained a hint of ethical rebuke. Commenting on the "monotonous, clumsy" second movement Trio, Schenker wrote "in music there are not only beautiful and unbeautiful thoughts, but also good and bad."[16] Schenker concluded, "thought-substance [*Gedankenmaterial*] of worth – of goodness and beauty – is forfeited by such bad presentation. And in this sense, I say, all of Bruckner's works are, despite their . . . entirely singular flights of symphonic fancy, simply badly written."[17]

Sustained discussion of the musical substance of the Eighth Symphony has always been quite rare, yet in the 1920s two sympathetic music analysts wrote extended essays on the work. Ernst Kurth discussed the symphony in depth in his extraordinary study, *Bruckner*. Kurth's exhaustive discussion (which covers sixty-five pages) cuts an unusual path between technical analysis and metaphorical exegesis; it traces the entire symphony with sparing recourse to analytical terminology, or even musical examples, yet succeeds in explicating the phenomenal progress of the music's unfolding with acute perspicacity.[18] Hugo Leichtentritt wrote an extensive essay on the Eighth (which was incorporated into the third and subsequent editions of his *Musikalische Formenlehre*) that was designed to complement Kurth's analysis by detailing the "technical, structural features of the symphony" not covered in the earlier author's "philosophical, aesthetic" study.[19] Kurth and Leichtentritt differed in their choice of emphasis – Kurth was far more interested in metaphysical symbolism, Leichtentritt more willing to provide detailed harmonic explanation – yet both essays, with their length and detail, respected the ineluctable complexity of symphonic meaning and resisted the urge to substitute verbal formulas for musical experience.

In the 1930s the landscape of Bruckner interpretation changed fundamentally. During this decade, the first modern collected edition of Bruckner's works, edited by Robert Haas, set out to present the world, for the first time, with the "pure" and "true" texts of Bruckner's music.[20] Haas's version of the Eighth Symphony (1939) differed radically from the previously available editions, and was based on questionable philology (see Appendix A). Also, in the Third Reich Anton Bruckner's image and his symphonies were appropriated as symbols of the Nazi ideal of German art and as a result the *völkisch* tendencies that had long colored the support Bruckner received in some quarters magnified terribly. In 1939, for example, Haas willfully described the Eighth in terms of contemporary cultural politics. He claimed the symphony as the "transfiguration" of the "deutscher Michel-Mythos," and suggested that this myth was finally reaching historical reality with the emergence of the "idea of greater Germany [*der großdeutschen Idee*]." Haas concluded that this aspiration was embodied by the fact that the "restored score [i.e., his edition] could ring out as a greeting from Ostmark [the Nazi term for Austria] precisely in this year": a transparently political statement a year after the annexation of Austria (and weeks after the occupation of Haas's native Czechoslovakia).[21]

After the War, when the ideological complicity of the fascist (and the earlier proto-fascist) Bruckner tradition seemed all too clear, commentators properly recoiled from the legacy of Nazi-era Bruckner criticism, and effectively broke with many of the interpretive approaches that had prevailed in previous decades. (In the process, many early twentieth-century connections were also severed and the tradition of Bruckner interpretation cut by the divide of the 1930s.) Partly because of this, the highly charged, impassioned partisanship that the Eighth inspired in its first half-century of existence waned.[22] Modern scholars have, with a few notable exceptions, been most comfortable addressing such relatively cool topics as textual criticism and formal analysis while leaving aside the passionate concern nineteenth-century critics had for the musical value and spiritual significance of Bruckner's symphonies. In other ways too modern Bruckner reception exhibits an ahistorical mien. Modern notions of editorial propriety have prompted us to forget all too well the text of the Eighth Symphony that was known in Bruckner's time. Current approaches to the performance of Bruckner's works similarly show little concern with history.

We face special problems, then, in placing the Eighth Symphony. For various reasons, many latter-day critics and scholars have been tempted to play Bruckner's advocate and treat his music with sympathy so deferential that it courts condescension, and posthumously balance the critical ledger. Bruckner's music often therefore comes to us wrapped in a cloak of historicist piety that paradoxically thwarts the pursuit of more meaningfully historical understanding. To think freshly and critically about the Eighth Symphony, or any of his works, requires the diligence, as Adorno wrote of Beethoven's *Missa Solemnis*, to "alienate it," to break through the crust of latter-day reception that "protectively surrounds it."[23] This can happen only if we are willing to prove our interpretations, and the ideas upon which they rest, against the historical density of the symphony's musical texts, its reception, and its original ideation.

2

The genesis and evolution of the Eighth Symphony

The arduousness of Bruckner's process of composition and, especially, his habits of revision are legendary; yet even by these standards, the Eighth Symphony had a long and difficult genesis and evolution. It was revised by the composer and exists in two distinct versions (1887 and 1890); the circumstances surrounding its revision were unusually complex; and its path to performance and publication was tortuous. This chapter chronicles the long journey of this symphony from its initial composition in 1884–7, through its rejection by Hermann Levi in October 1887, its recomposition by Bruckner in 1889 and 1890, and its performance and publication in 1892.

The composition of the first version

The Eighth Symphony originated between the summer of 1884 and August 1887, a time when Bruckner's career was reaching high tide. He had recently completed two of his most successful and powerful works, the Seventh Symphony and the *Te Deum*, both of which were published in 1885. While Bruckner was at work on the Eighth, the Seventh enjoyed a pair of triumphant initial performances in Leipzig on 30 December 1884 and in Munich on 10 March 1885 and several subsequent performances in Cologne, Chicago, Hamburg, New York, Amsterdam, Graz, Berlin, London, Dresden, and Budapest, as well as Vienna. The *Te Deum*, the Third Symphony (at that time the only other of Bruckner's symphonies available in print), and the String Quintet were also performed several times during these years. It was during this time of optimism and success that Bruckner set to work on the Eighth Symphony. He sketched the first movement in August 1884 in the cathedral town of Kremsmünster during his habitual summer sojourn in Upper Austria

Table 2.1 *The composition, revision, and publication of the Eighth Symphony*

Composition of the first version: July 1884 through August 1887

Summer 1884	composition of the first movement
November 1884 – February 1885	composition of the Adagio
23 July – 16 August 1885	composition of the Scherzo and Finale
September–October 1885	orchestration of Scherzo and first movement
February 1886	orchestration of first movement and Adagio
Summer 1886	Adagio installed as third movement
August–September 1886	orchestration of Adagio and Finale
March–April 1887	orchestration of Finale is completed
July–August 1887	finalization of first version and copying of a finished score
September/October 1887	Levi's rejection of the first version

Preparation of the second version: March 1889 – January 1890

March–May 1889	revision of the Adagio
July 1889	revision of the Finale
September 1889	revision of the Scherzo and Trio
November 1889	revision of the first movement
29 January 1890	Bruckner declares "last note written"
February 1890	copy of score prepared by Christ

Publication and performance: 1890–2

March 1890	Emperor Franz Joseph accepts the dedication of the Eighth Symphony
October 1890 – March 1891	preparations for Weingartner's planned performance
Summer 1891	preparation of score for publication
March 1892	Haslinger-Schlesinger-Lienau publishes the full score
18 December 1892	first performance, Vienna Philharmonic under Richter

(see Table 2.1).[1] Bruckner's faculty duties at the University of Vienna and the Vienna Conservatory severely limited his compositional activities during the academic year; thus, like Mahler a generation later, Bruckner composed primarily during the summer. By late September

1884 when Bruckner returned to Vienna to resume teaching the movement was fully drafted in short score, and on 23 September he played through it on the piano for Josef Schalk and Robert Hirsch.[2] The Adagio (which was originally planned as the second movement) was drafted between November 1884 and February 1885, with an interruption for his trip to Leipzig at the end of December to attend the first performance of his Seventh Symphony. He then left off work on the Eighth until the summer.

Bruckner returned to the work with renewed energy upon his arrival in Steyr in late July 1885. On 7 July 1885 he wrote to Arthur Nikisch that he intended to work "quickly."[3] He did. He drafted the Scherzo and Trio in the space of only four days (23–6 July) and immediately began to compose the Finale, which was largely drafted by 1 August and finished later that month. It is remarkable to note that the opening of this movement, which in its final form opens on a harmonically remote F♯, was first conceived, and sketched at some length, beginning on F♮.[4] The completed draft of the final pages of the Finale is signed: "Steyr, Stadtpfarrhof 16 August 1885. A. Bruckner. Halleluja!"[5] Later that same day, Bruckner reported enthusiastically to Franz Schalk that "the Eighth Symphony is just now finished [but only] in draft (alas). The Finale is the most significant movement of my life."[6]

Although extremely few sketch materials from Bruckner's previous works are extant, many drafts and sketches for the Eighth Symphony are preserved (the Österreichische Nationalbibliothek alone has more than thirty items containing sketches, drafts, and fragments of the work).[7] These include not only continuity drafts and compositional scores, but also a number of early sketches, which provide a rare opportunity to glimpse Bruckner's compositional methods. Bruckner devoted considerable effort to exploring the compositional potential of motivic and thematic ideas; he worked at length, for example, with the main theme of the finale, trying out the theme itself and its bass in various contrapuntal combinations, worked in canon, inverted, in diminution, set in contrary motion variation, and so forth.[8] Bruckner's first sketch of the Adagio is fascinating in this respect; these twelve measures contain the kernel of much of the completed movement (see Example 2.1). Some elements are already quite fully formed, notably the opening motive, with its dotted rhythm, chromatic neighbor-note figure, and its juxtaposition of tonic

Example 2.1 Early sketch of the Adagio, December 1884

NB: Bruckner often did not notate key signatures in his sketches, but rather indicated keys verbally (e.g., Des dur [D♭ major]). This transcription supplies the key signatures Bruckner indicated. The signature for F♯ minor seems to apply as early as m. 5.

source: A-Wn Mus. Hs. 6050

after Göllerich and Auer 4/2, 537 and Röthig (1978), 330

major and tonic minor. The rising sixth is also already present (Example 2.1, m. 4) but the scalewise descent that follows in the final version is here only adumbrated. The second half of the sketch contains a germinal version of the culmination of the opening thematic group. Measures 7 and 8 of the sketch show the rising arpeggio figure (already on A) that was to become mm. 15–17 of the finished movement, although in the sketch this figure is more static than it was to become, lacking as it does both the quintuplet turn figure and the conclusive scalar ascent to the high A it later gained (compare Example 3.8). Measures 9–12 of the sketch, on the other hand, are extremely similar to the final text (save for the extraneous B♭ in m. 12). This sketch also contains some elements that were to appear subsequently in rather different form and context. The rhythm and contour of m. 5 supplied the motivic basis of the second thematic group of the Adagio (beginning in m. 47 in the 1890 version), and the dissonant superimposition of D♮ above the tonic D♭/C♯ that is so important in the finished movement already hovers about the music (mm. 5–7). Here Bruckner's compositional process works out from the first *Einfall*; it was a matter of sorting out the elements and giving them effective shape, whether that meant simply sharpening them (as with the A major arpeggio), using them as the basis for a separate thematic section (as with the motive in m. 5 of the sketch), or developing their tonal and harmonic potential (as with the D/C♯ opposition).

Bruckner soon began to convert his short-score drafts into a full orchestral score. Between late August and October 1885 he orchestrated the Trio and began to score the Scherzo (which was still the third movement). He then began the score of the first movement, but only reached the middle of the movement (rehearsal K), before he broke off work on the project. In February he returned to finish the first movement and began to orchestrate the Adagio, which was still in place as the second movement. Again his work was interrupted until August, when, back in Steyr, he completed the score of the Adagio, which was now finally installed as the third movement, and moved on to the Finale.[9] He worked briefly on the orchestration of the Finale in September and October 1886, but soon temporarily stopped. On 16 November 1886 he wrote to Hermann Levi in a mood tinged by resignation and weariness: "I still don't know when the Eighth Symphony will be finished; after all, I have seven other symphonies."[10] He returned to the project later that winter; on 23 February 1887 in a letter to Elisabeth Kietz he explained why his correspondence had flagged: "It is the Eighth... So little time to work! It makes me desperate."[11] He finished the score of the Finale on 22 April 1887.[12]

In the summer of 1887, once again back in Upper Austria, Bruckner reviewed his manuscript one last time and had a copy of the score prepared by Karl Aigner, one of his local copyists.[13] The copying was finished on 9 August. By then Bruckner had begun to sketch the first movement of his Ninth Symphony.

The Levi affair

On 4 September 1887, soon after the copy of the score was finished, Bruckner wrote to Hermann Levi in Munich: "Hallelujah! The Eighth is finally ready and 'mein künstlerischer Vater' [my artistic father] must be the first to know . . . I would like to ask you, noble sir, for the [first] performance of the Eighth."[14] Levi responded with interest, and on 19 September Bruckner sent him the score. The accompanying note enthused: "May it find favor! My joy at the anticipated performance given by your noble, masterful hands is quite indescribable."[15] Upon studying the score, however, Levi concluded that he was unable to perform it. Bruckner, understandably deeply dismayed, withdrew from the work for some eighteen months, reworked it, and finally succeeded in having it published and performed in 1892.

The story of Hermann Levi's rejection of the first version of the Eighth Symphony is customarily told as a tragic tale: the conductor's refusal to perform the symphony staggers the composer who, with fractured confidence, proceeds to revise not only the work in question but several others over the course of several years. Commonly these revisions are judged ill-advised and ineffective, and are blamed for diverting Bruckner from further composition of other potentially important works. (Some writers have even mawkishly suggested that in this way the Levi affair was ultimately responsible for Bruckner's failure to complete his Ninth Symphony.[16]) This story needs to be revisited. Not only has our view of Bruckner's personality and biography evolved away from old images of beset genius, but important new evidence – notably Levi's long-lost letter to Bruckner explaining his response to the score – has turned up recently.

Levi and Bruckner first became acquainted at the Bayreuth Festivals of 1882 and 1884, and in 1884 Bruckner arranged to have a score of the Seventh Symphony sent to the conductor. Levi wrote that initially the work "took me aback, then fascinated me, and finally I developed tremendous respect for the man who could have created something so unusual and significant" (although, as he later admitted, he long remained rather befuddled by the Finale).[17] On 10 March 1885 in Munich Levi conducted the symphony, which had received its premiere in Leipzig under Nikisch in December 1884. This concert was the greatest triumph Bruckner had yet experienced; he was called to the stage by applause after each movement and the work was received warmly by the Munich press. On the following day at the Hoftheater, Levi indulgently replaced the scheduled opera, Nessler's *Der Trompeter von Säckingen*, with Bruckner's beloved *Die Walküre*. Levi further honored his guest when the performance was over; he had the brass section play the "Trauermusik" from the coda of the Adagio of the Seventh Symphony three times.[18] The following day featured a performance, again organized by Levi, of Bruckner's Quintet for Strings.

Levi also aided Bruckner in less direct ways, often making good use of his connections to the Bavarian Court. After performing the Seventh Symphony, Levi helped arrange for its publication. Not only did he intercede on Bruckner's behalf to help secure King Ludwig II's acceptance of the dedication but he was instrumental in raising the subvention required by the publisher, Albert Gutmann. In 1886 he worked to secure publication of Bruckner's Fourth Symphony (again with Gutmann), and again Levi raised the funds to pay the publisher's fee. In July 1886 Bruckner was awarded the *Ritterkreuz* of the Order of Franz Joseph (which brought with it an annuity of 300 florins) and again Levi's influence was helpful. The primary instigator of this award was Princess Amélie of Bavaria, who had been deeply moved by Levi's performance of Bruckner's *Te Deum* on 7 April 1886 and was quite taken by Bruckner himself. She expressed her enthusiasm to the conductor, and in a long letter Levi endorsed Amélie's assessment of Bruckner's great artistic importance and suggested that he might well merit royal support.[19] Thus emboldened, she wrote to the Austrian Archduchess Marie Valerie, the youngest daughter of Franz Joseph, who proposed the idea of honoring Bruckner with the *Ritterkreuz*.[20] Bruckner recognized Levi's role in this award and wrote to him: "I have received the order of Franz Joseph and 300 florins annually! This is your work, Herr Hofkapellmeister! I know it for certain! Eternal thanks from the bottom of my heart!"[21] Levi again offered decisive support for the honorary doctorate awarded to Bruckner by the University of Vienna in 1891. Asked about Bruckner's significance as a composer, Levi responded with a testimonial that sang Bruckner's praises very boldly: "Bruckner is, in my view, by far the most important symphonist of the post-Beethovenian period."[22] Obviously Levi was a vigorous intercessor or, as Bruckner himself put it, his "noblest benefactor [*edelsten Gönner*]."[23]

Levi had long been interested in the prospect of Bruckner's Eighth Symphony and in light of the tremendous support he had offered Bruckner during the composition of the work, it is little surprise that the composer offered him the first performance. Things did not turn out as either man would have wished. Levi's response to the work is remarkable, both in its musical judgments and for its genuine concern with Bruckner's feelings. He wrote first to Josef Schalk:

> Simply put: I cannot find myself in the Eighth Symphony and do not have the courage to perform it. The orchestra and the public will, of this I am certain, offer great resistance . . . I am terribly disappointed! I've studied it for days and can't make it my own. Far be it from me to pass judgment – it is possible that I'm deluded, that I'm too old or too dumb – but I find the instrumentation impossible and what has especially alarmed me is the great similarity with the Seventh; it virtually copies the form. The beginning of the first movement is grandiose, but with the development I don't know where to begin.
>
> And the last movement – it is a closed book to me.
>
> What to do now! I dread the thought of the effect this report will have on our friend. I can't write to him. Shall I suggest to him that he might hear the work in rehearsal here? In my desperation I have given the score to a musician here who's a good friend, and he also believes that a performance is impossible. Please write to me *immediately* about how I should act with Bruckner. When all is done, if he considers me an ass or, what would be worse, a traitor [*einen Treulosen*], I can accept it. But I fear worse, that this disappointment will completely crush him . . . Help me, I don't know what to do![24]

In a letter that is now lost Schalk advised Levi to write directly to Bruckner, and on 7 October Levi did so, pronouncing his opinion of the Eighth Symphony and informing the composer that he could not perform it. This letter was unknown for many years – Levi's draft copy of the letter was only recently unearthed in Munich by Laurence Dreyfus – and in the absence of Schalk's letter to Levi it was commonly assumed that Levi conveyed his message to Bruckner indirectly through Schalk. Now we can see that Levi did indeed directly inform Bruckner of his opinion of the work, and that he communicated what was obviously a very painful decision with admirable frankness.[25]

Dear and revered friend,

For the last 8 days already I have been occupied with writing you (in my mind) long letters. Never in my life have I found it so difficult to find the right words for what I need to say! But it can't be put off any longer . . .

So: I find it impossible to perform the Eighth in its current form. I just can't make it my own! As much as the themes are magnificent and direct, their working-out seems to me dubious; indeed, I consider the orchestration quite impossible . . . The performance of the Eighth in a subscription concert would be a risk which, in your interest, I must not take . . . I have pored over the score for hours, yea days, but I have not come closer to the work . . . Release me from my promise to perform the work, I would certainly conduct it badly, too, let me put on the Romantic [i.e., the Fourth Symphony] in November! — — Write to me soon — whatever it is — but do let me know what you make of these lines, which have taken a lot out of me! Don't lose your courage, take another look at your work, talk it over with your friends, with Schalk, maybe a reworking can achieve something — Keep me in your good books! Consider me an ass, I don't mind, but don't think that my feelings for you have changed in any way or could ever do so.[26]

Levi heard nothing from Bruckner for a week. Understandably worried, he wrote to Schalk on 14 October: "I wrote to Bruckner, but have not yet received any reply. Has he spoken to you or perhaps shown you my letter? How has he taken it? Please go to see him and let me know how you find him."[27] Schalk responded four days later with a letter that has spawned more than its share of speculation:

Your report has understandably hit Professor Bruckner very hard. He feels eternally unlucky and will hear no words of consolation. It [your response] was expected and was the gentlest way of preventing him from bitter disappointments. I hope that he will soon settle down and undertake a revision of the work at your advice . . . At the moment certainly he had best not work [on it], since he is upset and despairs of himself and does not feel capable of anything. However, with his colossal natural power, physical as well as moral, he will be back to it soon . . . One must let him calm down by himself. In any case, he is indebted to you for your frank evaluation, which saved him from great failure and, even if he cannot see it yet, the time for it will come.[28]

In just two days Bruckner responded to Levi with a short letter:

Only now do I have the time to study the matter. I'll do what is possible – to the best of my knowledge and belief. When at last all is done, I will ask you to lead a few rehearsals, at my expense, with your Hoforchester before the Princess [Amélie], whom I will need in this case, as you well know.[29]

Bruckner's wounded pride is not hard to detect in his curt tone and his grudging acceptance that the work might benefit from further "study." His residual stubbornness is also evident in his suggestion that he might finance some orchestral rehearsals, presumably in the hope that this might demonstrate to Levi that the symphony would actually come across effectively in performance. Bruckner was not, as Levi feared (and as many later writers have asserted), utterly crushed by his friend's negative judgment of the Eighth. He was staggered by the blow, yet with his inner resiliency and his great determination, he rallied. By 23 October he had regained enough self-confidence to question privately Levi's capacity for judgment; Princess Amélie recorded that Bruckner said to her that "Levi – he's a knave [*Schlankl*]. It's hard for him to grasp things, you know."[30]

It took Bruckner some time to reconcile himself to the need to revise. He looked over the score in late 1887, and by the end of January 1888 he seems to have accepted that he must revise the work.[31] On 30 January he wrote to his friend Betty von Mayfeld that "the Eighth Symphony is far from done" and needed "major alterations"[32] and on 4 February in a letter to Levi primarily concerned with a planned performance of the Fourth Symphony on 14 April 1888, he mentioned, almost incidentally, "I certainly have reason to be ashamed of myself – at least this time – because of the Eighth. I am an ass. Now I see things differently."[33]

The question of why and how Bruckner began to see the Eighth differently needs detailed explication, and is the subject of Chapter 5. For the moment, suffice it to say that while Levi's rejection of the symphony undoubtedly played a decisive part, Bruckner's eventual revision cannot fairly be described as a simplification or mollification of his original conception nor can it reasonably be seen as an attempt to make the score acceptable to Levi or even to other potential performers and listeners. If this was Bruckner's intention, he failed: Levi never did perform the symphony and even in its revised version the work presented prohibitive technical difficulties for many orchestras.

Bruckner's revision

During the winter of 1887–88 Bruckner had been occupied with the preparation of the final version of the Fourth Symphony and its performance by the Vienna Philharmonic on 22 January 1888, and he spent the remainder of the year working on the final revision of the Third Symphony. It was not until 4 March 1889, the very day on which he finished the revision of the Third Symphony, that the composer began the actual task of revising the Eighth. He began by reworking the Adagio and finished on 8 May.[34] He then turned his attention to the Finale and completed its revision on 31 July 1889. In revising this movement Bruckner worked directly on his autograph score from 1887, and wrote in changes, crossed out passages, and inserted new pages as necessary.[35] He next revised the second movement, finishing the Scherzo in Steyr on 4 September (his sixty-fifth birthday) and the Trio, which was extensively rewritten, on 25 September.[36] (This was the only movement of the revised version that Bruckner wrote out entirely in his own hand.) In November 1889, back in Vienna, he began work on the first movement, and used, as he had with the Adagio, a copy of the movement from 1887 in the hand of Hofmeyer.[37] The revision of this movement moved more slowly, probably because of the extent of the revisions as well as the demands of Bruckner's teaching. Bruckner noted at the end of the score "last note written" on 29 January 1890, yet he continued to tinker with the movement in February. Finally, on 10 March he signed and dated the score with the remark "entirely finished" and on 14 March he ran through the movement one last time.[38] When the composition was complete, Bruckner had two clean copies of the score prepared by his copyists.[39]

Dedication and publication

Bruckner long planned to dedicate the Eighth to the Emperor; in his letter to Levi announcing the completion of the first version of the Eighth (4 September 1887) he stated that he planned "to request that the Emperor accept the dedication; then Richter has promised (since my plan pleases him) to give a performance" in Vienna.[40] When the revised score was ready, Bruckner promptly wrote to Emperor Franz Joseph II requesting permission to dedicate the symphony to him.[41] Much to Bruckner's satisfaction, the Emperor accepted the dedication and, in addition, volunteered a subvention of 3,000 florins to defray publication costs.[42] (Again Levi seems to have been involved behind the scenes. As early as 14 November 1886 he had written to Franz Schalk that Princess Amélie had informed him that the Emperor would pay for the cost of publication.[43])

Bruckner had always had difficulty getting his work into print. He struggled to find publishers and, when he did, was often displeased with their work. As a result, Bruckner's works were published piecemeal; he enjoyed nothing like, for example, Brahms's long relationship with Simrock or Verdi's with Ricordi, nor did he make more than token income from his publications. His Third Symphony was, unusually, published shortly after its premiere in December 1877. This came about quite fortuitously: Theodor Rättig, a fledgling music publisher who attended the first performance of the symphony and was among the small group enthused by the work, immediately offered to publish the score. Eventually he published two versions of the Third Symphony (1878 and 1890), the *Te Deum* (1885), and several smaller choral works. In the 1880s the Viennese impresario and publisher Albert J. Gutmann published Bruckner's Quintet (1884) and the Seventh and Fourth Symphonies (in 1885 and 1889 respectively), but Bruckner was satisfied with neither Gutmann's terms (he demanded a fee of 1,000 florins for each of the symphonies) nor his work, which tended to be sloppy and late. The difficulties Bruckner encountered with Gutmann in preparing the Seventh Symphony were great enough that Bruckner resolved never to work with the publisher again. He approached two German publishers, Schott (Mainz) and Bote & Bock (Berlin), with his Fourth Symphony, both of whom rejected it, before settling for Gutmann. Bruckner's misgivings about Gutmann proved well-founded. The first printing of the Fourth Symphony was ridden with so many errors that Bruckner compelled Gutmann to withdraw it and issue a corrected printing.[44]

It was during the composition of the Eighth Symphony, therefore, that Bruckner experienced his worst travails with Gutmann, and he never seems to have even considered offering this symphony to Gutmann. Instead, as soon as Franz Joseph had agreed to accept the dedication, Bruckner immediately began to talk about finding a publisher in Germany.[45] In a letter to Levi on 28 April 1890, Bruckner asked the conductor to support Bruckner's plan to have Schott publish the Eighth.[46] Bruckner held out hope for Schott as late as March 1891, but in the end they did not publish the score.[47] Bruckner did eventually succeed, at least in part, in finding a German publisher. In late 1890 the firm of Haslinger–Schlesinger–Lienau, which was based in Berlin but had an important branch in Vienna as a result of its incorporation of the Viennese firm of Haslinger in 1875, agreed to publish the symphony. The score was prepared for publication in mid-1891; the proofreading and correction were done by Bruckner's student Max von Oberleithner (1868–1935), who also seems to have contributed financially.[48] (For example, Oberleithner guaranteed the sale of 200 copies of the four-hand arrangement of the symphony and in exchange Lienau agreed to let Josef Schalk, and not the house arranger, prepare the score. This total was reached with the aid of Hugo Kaun, a Bruckner devotee and conductor in Milwaukee [!][49]) The published score of the Eighth Symphony was issued in March 1892, and thus became the only one of Bruckner's symphonies to be published before it had been performed.

Bringing the symphony to performance

Just as Bruckner struggled to have his works published, for much of his career he had difficulty in securing performances of his symphonies, and by the time of the Eighth Symphony, Bruckner's music was only just beginning to win its way onto orchestral programs. The slowness with which Bruckner's works entered the repertory is often ascribed to the conservatism, even philistinism, of orchestral establishments. There is some truth in this charge; certainly many orchestras were disinclined to perform such "modern" music, especially as part of their subscription concerts, which tended to be dominated by old-guard audiences.[50] Beyond these matters of musical taste, Bruckner's symphonies presented great technical and practical challenges to orchestras. Concern about audience reaction and the difficulty of the orchestral writing were evident in Levi's response to the first version of the Eighth Symphony: he wrote that in his judgment because of "the possible effect on an audience like my own . . . the performance of the Eighth in a subscription concert would be a risk which, in your interest, I must not take" and found "the orchestration quite impossible" and worried that Bruckner's "sense for beauty and balance and euphony has somewhat suffered. How else could your treatment of the trumpets and tubas (really of the winds in general) be explained!"[51] Levi wrote that even with the rather easier

Seventh Symphony, "the orchestra started to become impatient, indeed . . . voices were raised suggesting the work be removed from the repertory." In other words, Levi felt that the Seventh Symphony strained the limit of the practically possible, while the Eighth Symphony overstepped it. (This conclusion is quite remarkable for the man who only five years earlier had given the first performances of *Parsifal*, a work that would seem to be at least as challenging in all ways.)

Even after Bruckner revised the score, practical difficulties and stylistic doubts continued to hamper the dissemination of the Eighth Symphony. By this time, Levi was no longer conducting concerts in Munich and was thus not in a position to perform it himself. Levi was apparently not particularly interested in promoting the Eighth Symphony, in any case; although he was able to arrange a concert of the Fourth Symphony in Munich on 10 December 1890 (conducted by his assistant Franz Fischer), the Eighth was not performed in Munich during Levi's tenure there. Instead Levi recommended it to the young Felix Weingartner (1863–1942), who had assisted him at Bayreuth and who had recently been appointed Kapellmeister in Mannheim. Weingartner was intrigued by the idea, and on 14 September 1890 he wrote to Levi, "Dear Papa, have you written to Bruckner regarding his Eighth? . . . If Bruckner sends me the parts, then I'll certainly perform the symphony and soon, in the second or third concert, but he mustn't give it to anyone else first. This is a condition."[52] Levi wrote apologetically to Bruckner that he could not do the Eighth ("you must consider me a swindler") but that Weingartner was interested.[53] Bruckner accepted Weingartner's proposal (he even boasted, possibly fancifully, that he had "refused" Richter in favor of Weingartner) and arranged to have the orchestral parts copied in Mannheim and had a score sent to Weingartner.[54] The concert was eventually scheduled for 26 March 1891 and was to feature Beethoven's Second Symphony and the first performance of Hugo Wolf's "Christnacht" in addition to the Eighth Symphony.

On 20 March Weingartner informed Bruckner that he had to postpone the concert until 2 April, owing to the Good Friday performance of the *St. Matthew Passion* on 27 March.[55] At the last minute, however, Weingartner removed the Eighth Symphony from the program and replaced it with Liszt's *Dante Symphony*. On 9 April he wrote to Bruckner that his appointment as conductor of the Königliche Oper in Berlin had been "so sudden and the change in my position so unexpected" that it had disrupted his schedule and prevented him from rehearsing the symphony adequately and would moreover obviously mean that he would not have another chance to do the symphony in the foreseeable future.[56] The previous day he had written to Levi more frankly:

> Unfortunately I couldn't perform the Bruckner. The symphony offers such difficulties that I could not demand the necessary rehearsals. We had new tuba players who were not experienced enough in their instruments . . . I clarified the circumstances to Bruckner. He seemed to be understanding and sees no harm as Richter will immediately perform it in London [this performance never materialized]. The sonorous effect of the Eighth Symphony is unfortunately offensively raw . . . [57]

Of course, Bruckner deduced the truth; he wrote to Levi on 18 April: "I think that the symphony did not please Herr Weingartner or sounded poorly [*schlecht geklungen*]."[58]

Although Weingartner's performance did not come to pass, it occasioned some of the most important – and most widely misinterpreted – of Bruckner's comments on the symphony. On 27 January 1891 Bruckner sent Weingartner a letter containing a sporadically detailed, extramusical program for the symphony (see Chapter 3).[59] Even more famously, Bruckner's correspondence about the performance makes mention of cuts in the Finale. His initial note to Weingartner (2 October 1890) contains a brief postscript: "The Finale has [indications for] large cuts; please shorten it because of its lengthiness."[60] The specific cuts Bruckner suggested are unknown, but they undoubtedly included one indicated in a loose page inserted into the manuscript (mm. 345–86 of the 1890 version).[61] In his letter on 27 January 1891, by which time Bruckner seems to have been growing uneasy with the entire affair, he reiterated that Weingartner should "please shorten the Finale as indicated; it would be far too long and is valid only for later times and for a circle of friends and connoisseurs [*gilt nur späteren Zeiten und zwar für einen Kreis von Freunden und Kennern*]."[62] On Good Friday, 27 March 1891, Bruckner again urged Weingartner to "please accept the cuts in the finale, since otherwise it would be too long." More interestingly, he also requested that Weingartner not physically alter the score and wrote that "it is one of my dearest wishes" that the orchestral parts remain unaltered for publication.[63]

24

Much has been made of these comments; the phrase "for later times and for a circle of friends and connoisseurs" in particular has been adopted as a motto by those who believe that the early editions of Bruckner are corrupt. Since the 1930s it has been claimed as a sign that Bruckner privately wished that the so-called "original versions" of his works eventually be published.[64] In considering the validity of this interpretation, it should be borne in mind that although Bruckner's request has almost always been read as if it referred to the autograph manuscript, it did not. The score that Weingartner had in his possession was a copy made by Victor Christ, probably the one made in 1890.[65] It is probable, in fact, that the manuscript Weingartner had in his possession was the one eventually used in the preparation of the printed edition of 1892; not only does Bruckner's concern that the score and parts not actually be altered presuppose that they would eventually be used by the publisher, but we know that a copy made by Christ and Hofmeyr was the actual *Stichvorlage* (see Chapter 6). Bruckner's allusion to posterity therefore has nothing to do with the earlier version of the symphony – even less does it encode a wish for a posthumous edition based on his unpublished manuscript scores. His concern was simpler: he wanted to ensure that his revised score be printed without the actual excision of the passages he asked Weingartner to cut and without any alterations to the scoring made in rehearsal by Weingartner. Thus Bruckner seems, perhaps ironically in light of later interpretations, to have believed that the late revised version – and not the putative "Originalfassung" – was meant for later generations of connoisseurs.

Bruckner was stung by the fiasco with Weingartner. Even a year later, on 22 April 1892, he wrote to Levi: "What I suffered in Vienna because of the Eighth – I will remain silent for now. I conceived of performance only by you, certainly not the little orchestra with military tubas (!!!) and the (in my eyes) suspicious Herr Weingartner in Mannheim. Now a year is lost!"[66] Although Levi no longer regularly conducted the orchestral concerts in Munich, Bruckner clearly wanted him to perform the Eighth; on 24 July 1892 Bruckner played his trump card, Wagner's personal pledge to perform his symphonies: "Perhaps I can hope that my *künstl. Vater* will perform my Eighth Symphony once in Munich in one of his special concerts, as the noblest advocate of our immortal, blessed *Meister*, who also, as he assured me, wished to perform my symphonies."[67] Levi apparently agreed – presumably somewhat grudgingly – to do either the Seventh or the Eighth Symphony at the Tonkünstlerfest of the Allgemeiner deutscher Musikverein scheduled for Munich in September 1892.[68] These plans came to nothing: the festival was relocated to Vienna, and finally canceled because of a feared cholera outbreak.[69] Levi was, for whatever reason, not willing to perform the Eighth himself; as late as 12 January 1892, after the successful performance in Vienna, he wrote to Bruckner that he still did not have the "courage" to do the Eighth.[70]

Bruckner realized well before this time that Levi was not going to champion the Eighth and instead focused his efforts on arranging a performance in Vienna. As Josef Schalk wrote on 29 January 1892, "Bruckner is going at it with all seriousness to produce a performance of the Eighth."[71] At last Hans Richter, whom Bruckner had pointedly bypassed five years before in favor of Levi and two years before in favor of Weingartner, agreed to give the first performance, and on 18 December 1892, the Eighth Symphony was finally performed at a subscription concert of the Vienna Philharmonic. Despite the success of its premiere, the symphony was slow to gain widespread acceptance. It was performed only twice more before Bruckner's death, in Olmütz (Olomouc) under Vladimir Labler on 22 October 1893 and by Jean-Louis Nicodé in Dresden on 18 December 1895. The first performance in Munich was conducted by Siegmund von Hausegger on 17 December 1900, some seven months after Levi's untimely death. The second performance by the Vienna Philharmonic was on 21 October 1906 under Bruckner's old protégé Franz Schalk. The Eighth was first played in America by the Boston Symphony Orchestra under Max Fiedler on 12 March 1909.

3

The musical design and symphonic agenda of the Eighth

In the final decades of the nineteenth century the symphony was a loaded genre, both culturally and compositionally. Beethoven's great examples, especially the *Eroica*, the Fifth, and the Ninth, had long since secured the symphony as the highest, most elevated, and most meaningful genre of instrumental music. Yet, despite its cultural prestige, symphonic composition was beset by special challenges in the late nineteenth century. A *sine qua non* of the symphony during this era was monumentality, a trait that was essential to the public significance of the genre in an age given to bourgeois expansiveness and increasing rationalization, in which the construction of historical memory (which is what monuments do) increasingly substituted for religion and myth.[1] During this period many progressive composers, including Bruckner, also desired to enrich the symphony with an infusion of "Wagnerian" vocabulary. Gustav Mahler put it simply: "Wagner took over the *expressive means* of symphonic music, just as now the symphonist will lay claim in his turn to the expressive riches gained for music through Wagner's efforts."[2] This desire to win some of Wagner's "expressive riches" for the symphony raised something of a compositional puzzle. Monumentality presupposes grandeur, solidity, massiveness; therefore, a crucial task of the symphonist was to find ways of articulating large, coherent formal spans, which rested upon strong tonal and metrical frameworks, out of harmonic and motivic substance that was weighted toward expressive detail and pointed characterization and thus prone to fragmentation. Posed in these terms, a central concern of Bruckner's symphonic project can be seen as a working-out of this synthesis and the construction of grand monumental symphonies that, as Norbert Nägler wrote, "tectonically sublimate" Wagner's chromaticism and "endless melody."[3] Thus it was given to Bruckner "as purifier of Wagner," in Ernst Bloch's words,

27

finally to separate "the benefits of the Wagnerian style, 'eloquent' music, from the penalties of the programme or the music drama and to have thus internalised it. . . as the route to other waters than those of poetry."[4]

Movement 1: Allegro moderato

The first movement, like all of Bruckner's opening movements, is built around the established framework of sonata form. The scheme of exposition, development, and recapitulation is easily discerned, and the overall structure palpably enacts the tonal drama of sonata form. Indeed, a bird's-eye view of the movement shows clear formal divisions; upon closer examination, however, any hint of formal conventionality recedes and what Dahlhaus called the "radical nature of [Bruckner's] compositional technique" grows increasingly vivid.[5] Particularly impressive is the virtuosity with which Bruckner harnesses a centrifugal, chromatic harmonic vocabulary for the purpose of building a tonally closed symphonic form.[6] In doing so, Bruckner performs a delicate harmonic balancing act. The tonic key of C minor is effectively defined by the tonal articulations of the movement, yet many passages – and not only developmental ones – eschew standard harmonic syntax in favor of elaborate chromatic motion. Bruckner reserves clearly defined cadential progressions (i.e., those in which, in Schoenberg's definition, three successive chords "unmistakably express a region or tonality"[7]) for junctures that define the tonal framework of the movement.

The movement opens with an exposition consisting of three distinct thematic units of roughly equal length: the main thematic group (mm. 1–50), a contrasting thematic group in the dominant (mm. 51–96), and a closing section in E♭, the relative major (mm. 97–152). There follow a substantial development section (beginning in m. 153), a reprise of the second and third sections of the exposition (mm. 311–92), which unusually avoids solidly grounding the tonic key, and a compact coda (mm. 393–417). The recapitulation of the opening material bridges the end of the development and the return of the second thematic group in such a way that the crucial division of development and recapitulation – a juncture freighted with structural meaning – is artfully blurred (see Table 5.1, p. 73 below).

The remarkable opening pages immediately unsettle expectation. The tonality of the opening theme is at first quite indefinable; its most

Example 3.1 First movement, mm. 1–6

Example 3.2 First movement, mm. 9–21, harmonic progression

obvious tonal trait is that it is not in the movement's tonic key of C minor, or indeed any easily identifiable key (see Example 3.1). The striking use of G♭ and D♭ as chromatic neighbor tones, which will prove to be a crucial motive as the movement unfolds, both infuses the music with a charge of kinetic energy and clouds the latent suggestion of C minor accruing from the f′ followed by g′ sustained in the accompanying violins and horns, the arrival (under the g′) on C in m. 5, and (a bit more distantly) the clarinet fifth on the dominant in mm. 5–6. These provisional assertions of the tonic are swept away by the next dozen measures, which lead the opening motive through a stretch of roving harmony, the terminology coined by Schoenberg to describe chromatic progressions that do not employ standard harmonic syntax and "fail to express a tonality" (see Example 3.2).[8] In m. 17 the chromaticism begins to clear in preparation for a half cadence on the dominant of C minor. Closure onto the tonic triad is preempted by a sudden restatement of the opening material (m. 23) in full orchestral dress. Here the chromatic continuation is slightly different (mm. 28–39): it glances at the tonic (mm. 40–1), before arriving on the submediant, which then serves as the basis of an augmented-sixth progression (m. 43) that leads to the dominant, in which key the second theme group begins.

This passage does the typical work of a symphonic opening: presenting a protagonistic theme, exposing basic motives, and limning the tonic key. In addition, it establishes two principles that are important to the movement, and the symphony, as a whole. First, it introduces the tendency of harmonic complexity to give way to relative stability and consonance as the point of cadence nears, a pattern that recurs on various levels throughout the piece, as does the particular strategy of anchoring spans of elaborate unstable chromaticism with cadential assertions of a structural key, here the tonic, later also the dominant, the mediant, and other related keys. (The particular device, which was canonized in *Tristan*, of asserting a key by sounding its dominant seventh, even in the absence of its tonic triad as in mm. 21–2, also grows characteristic of the piece.) Second and more particularly, the prominence given to chromatic neighbor notes in the initial thematic unit (in mm. 3–5 and more forcefully in mm. 25–7) proves to be a basic motivic conceit. At many junctures of the movement structural tones – the tonic, dominant, and subdominant – play off in various ways with their chromatic neighbors; sometimes this happens with little moment (e.g., in the course of the second theme group) and sometimes with tremendous structural drama, as at the height of the development section.

The second thematic group begins with a sudden unclouded G major triad and a disarming tune (m. 51). This thematic group is based in G, and for all of its difference in mood and harmonic style (it is far more triadic), the tonal build of this section resembles that of its predecessor in one important way. Its tonic is at first only loosely defined and is surrounded by wandering sequential syntax; not until the clearly defined cadential activity around the restatement of the tune in G (m. 73) is the key of the dominant solidified. The harmony also has a tendency to turn from G major to G♭ major and its cognates, thereby not only tonicizing a pitch that was prominent in the opening theme, but also working out in a new way the chromatic neighbor-note motive that opened the symphony.

The third thematic group introduces another strong contrast. It begins with a fresh, striding theme that quickly begins to describe the key of E♭, the mediant of C minor, and thus the conventional contrasting tonal pole in a minor-key sonata-form exposition. E♭ is initially given as a

Example. 3.3 First movement, mm. 183–7

minor key; the major is reserved until E♭ is regained after an intervening stretch of harmonic roving (m. 125). As in the two preceding thematic groups, cadentially secured harmonic poles anchor unstable chromatic harmony, although here the proportions are quite different and the structural key, E♭, is granted substantially greater weight. Fourteen measures are given to a very long dominant preparation of E♭, balanced by fourteen more that linger on the tonicized triad (mm. 125–52).

The development section is elaborate. It opens with an intense meditation on the opening motive during which the brass and winds make obvious play with the motive's distinctively plastic shape against a background of tremolando strings. These variants generally adhere quite closely to the original form of the motive, often preserving it intact but inverted (as in the woodwinds, mm. 169–71 and 179–81) or in inversion and augmentation (as in the brass, mm. 173–7 and 183–7). At other times the contour and pitch of the motive are changed more freely. These variations range from minor intervallic changes (horn, mm. 141–5) to revamping the contour (mm. 140–51 and trumpets, mm. 175–9). As if in compensation for its textural and motivic clarity, this episode rises to great harmonic intensity by collapsing the chromatic neighbor notes into implacably sustained dissonances (see Example 3.3).

This overt manipulation of the primary motivic material dramatizes a process that imbues much of the movement in a less obvious way. As Werner Korte pointed out, Bruckner's primary motives tend to be sharply profiled and highly distinctive, and the strategic exploitation of this "capacity for meaningful flexibility [*flexibler Mehrdeutigkeit*] and reinterpretation" assumes a formative, structural function in

Example 3.4 First movement, mm. 3–21, motivic "mutation"

After Korte (1963), 27

Bruckner's symphonies. Korte called this process, by which "decisive [motivic] traits are changed suddenly in favor of new ones," mutation.[9] In the process, as Dahlhaus later pointed out, the parameters of rhythm and pitch are separated and abstracted from "'concrete' motives" and are treated as self-standing elements "unconnected to each other, freed from their original formation."[10] These two parameters are handled differently: mutation almost always entails intervallic changes, while rhythmic features tend to be more stable. Thus rhythmic patterns become preeminent sources of continuity and coherence, while pitch structures continually evolve and develop. This is what happens in the opening bars of the movement (see Example 3.4). Measures 3–5 contain the basic idea, which immediately mutates in mm. 7–9. The rhythm is preserved intact, but the melodic contour is changed fundamentally. Some intervallic features are retained, notably the initial minor second, while others are recognizably modified, for example the chromatic tail of m. 4, which is inverted in m. 8 (and echoed by the oboe and clarinet in mm. 9–10, 13–14, and 17–18). (Other less obvious intervallic connections might be drawn as well, including the inversionally related leaps of a minor sixth [mm. 3–4] and major third [mm. 7–8] and the overall span of a minor third common to both m. 4 and m. 8.) The ensuing bars continue this process, each successive unit deriving from its predecessor, like links in a chain. The next segment (mm. 11–13) begins with a motivic minor second and a simple rhythmic modification, but the continuation introduces a new triplet rhythm and new melodic intervals. The next link (mm. 15–17) has the same rhythm, but new pitch content in its second half. At m. 18 the triplet motive is broken off and inverted as the music moves toward cadence.

As several scholars have shown in detail, the entire symphony is inhabited by densely interlocking networks of motivic similarities, from the intervallic parallels (chromatic ornaments and upward minor sixth) between the head-motives of the first movement and Adagio to the manifold uses of the rhythm of the initial motive of the symphony.[11] Modern notions of symphonic aesthetics are inclined to underrate the importance of these patterns of motivic integration, connection, and mutation, since now the essence of symphonic form is located primarily in formal and tonal architecture, not motivic connections. Yet in the latter half of the nineteenth century different standards of judgment prevailed, as we can see in Wagner's definition of "symphonic unity" as a "web of basic themes . . . which contrast, complete, re-shape, divorce, and intertwine with one another."[12] In Bruckner's symphonies this web is spun largely out of rhythm; recurring rhythmic cells and a solidly quadratic periodic structure endow the music with great tensile strength. This rhythmic and hyperrhythmic solidity, along with large-scale spans of tonal coherence, is the basis of Bruckner's symphonic structure; by undergirding surface features, notably locally modulatory harmony and vivid episodic contrasts, that might otherwise be prone to fragmentation, it allows the creation of symphonic forms that incorporate great contrasts, diverse moods, and fine detail into an epic structure.

Example 3.5 First movement, mm. 225–31

The development section continues with a statement of the main idea of the second thematic group in inversion beginning in G♭ (mm. 193–200). This quickly devolves into what initially appears to be the beginning of a forceful dominant preparation in C minor (mm. 201–12), which seems to herald a return to the tonic. Historically, composers have treated this juncture – which typically delivers both the tonic key and the main thematic material – as a crucial dramatic stroke. But in this movement Bruckner diffuses the process of recapitulation, both tonal and thematic, over the space of some seventy-five measures. Thus, as the dominant of C minor begins to gather itself, the harmony slips (not by the most obvious path) to the dominant of B♭ minor (mm. 217–24) and the music drives forward to a massive thematic statement that sets the opening theme, in the bass and low brass, below a clear variant of the second theme group, in the upper strings and woodwinds, with both elements rhythmically augmented to double their original value (see Example 3.5). Gesturally this feels like a recapitulation, and it does restate the opening theme at its original pitch level, yet the original theme itself deflects the tonic key, and Bruckner capitalizes on its tonal ambivalence.[13] He leans on the G♭ neighbor note heavily so that the harmonic weight veers away from the tonic, so much so that when the phrase arrives on C (m. 229) it feels provisional. Bruckner repeats this grandiose thematic unit twice, with each statement a third higher (starting on A♭ in m. 235 and on C in m. 245). (A close study will reveal that this passage masterfully throws the balance of harmonic tones and non-harmonic tones into controlled confusion; see especially mm. 225–8 and 235–8.) The final repetition comes to rest on G (m. 249) and this pitch –

Example 3.6 First movement, mm. 253–8

the dominant – holds, rooted by a long, quiet tonic pedal in the timpani (mm. 247–64), above which, in an oddly austere passage, two trumpets softly intone the bare rhythm of the main theme in octaves on the pitch C while a flute adds a descant outlining an octave and fifth on C as the basses descend nervously to low G again and again (see Example 3.6). The home tonality is thus reached, although without the usual cadential definition.

This harmonic stability dissolves into a passage (mm. 267–78) that quickly ascends through G♭ major, crests on the dominant ninth of C minor (with the trumpets again playing the motto rhythm, now on G, in mm. 271–8), and subsides by falling through a diminished seventh chord. The music resumes quietly on the dominant of D♭ (m. 279) and then, for the first time in the movement, the opening theme is sounded beginning on G (first oboe, mm. 283–5), the pitch level at which it most clearly rests within C minor (it circles around the minor sixth, G-E♭, that is part of the tonic triad). The long passage on C above the timpani pedal and the powerful assertion of the dominant have done enough to restore tonal centricity that this statement of the theme does not need to decide on the tonic key; indeed this is exactly what it avoids. The oboe is surrounded by filigrees outlining the dominant of D♭; this extraordinary harmonization not only realizes the C-D♭ opposition introduced in the opening bars, but again shifts the music away from the key of C. This movement away from the tonic continues in the ensuing elaboration (as does the play with chromatic neighbor notes), yet in this midst the strong cadential figure (outlining iv-i$^6_4$-V^7) that had punctuated the opening page of the movement returns squarely in C (mm. 300–2). This cadential gesture could easily usher in the entry on C minor, possibly with the opening theme or more likely the second thematic group; but while it does inaugurate the return of the second thematic group, this is not in the tonic key. Instead, the music slides through G♭ to an augmented sixth that leads to the key of E♭.

The second thematic group is restated in full in E♭, and the third thematic group begins in due course in the key of C minor. The initial section of this unit leads, as it did in the exposition, to a turbulent, harmonically unsettled continuation, but now it turns in a new direction. A strongly directed chromatic rise leads to a thunderous, aggressively diatonic peroration in C minor (mm. 369–84), built on a rising diatonic tetrachord and the resounding intonation of the motto rhythm on C by three trumpets and three horns. This tremendous magnification of the passage on C that occupied an earlier part of the recapitulatory space (mm. 250–62) elevates the hollowness of the earlier passage to the proportion of tragic grandeur. At its peak the orchestra drops out, dramatically exposing the three horns and three trumpets and leaving them to peal alone into the abyss. For all its loud emphasis of C, this passage is so strongly based on the tonic 6/4 chord (the timpani pedal on the tonic notwithstanding) that it forecloses a finally clinching tonal arrival. The music quickly wanes, and a quiet roll of the timpani leads to a compact, tensely immobile coda that gently unwinds the opening motive above an unwavering tonic pedal.

Movement 2: *Scherzo*: Allegro moderato; *Trio*: Langsam

Bruckner's Scherzi are outstanding for their freshness and rugged vigor, and this one is no exception. In the Eighth, the Scherzo does, however, function differently from those in Bruckner's previous symphonies. It is the second movement, rather than the third, and for the first time since the Third Symphony, it is placed in the tonic key. Thus rather than appearing as a strong contrast – in tempo, key, and tone – to a preceding slow movement, this Scherzo, in effect, joins with the opening Allegro to form the first part of the symphony.

Example 3.7 Scherzo, mm. 1–5

The movement follows the classical pattern of Scherzo, Trio, and *da capo* reprise of the Scherzo. The Scherzo is built almost exclusively out of two elements: a short string of chromatic, descending parallel sixth chords, and a squarely sturdy motive based on an arpeggiated tonic triad, which is solidly formed but not particularly expressive (Example 3.7). This arpeggio figure functions as the main-spring of the movement; it sets into motion an effortlessly steady forward flow that suffuses the whole Scherzo. As the music unrolls through superbly regular four-bar units (a pattern broken only by three six-bar phrases: mm. 19–24, 89–94, and 153–8), it is easy to feel it as a grand piece of symphonic clockwork.

The Scherzo is an expansive rounded binary form. The first half of the movement (mm. 1–64) moves from C minor to E♭, with mystery-making arrivals in A major, E major, and A♭ minor (mm. 33–6, 37–40, and 49–52, respectively) along the way. The second half of the movement opens with a developmental area that falls into several parts: a sequentially structured section dominated by diminished and half-diminished sonorities (mm. 65–90); a rather formal cadential preparation in C minor (mm. 91–4); a leisurely exploration of the inversion of the opening arpeggio figure (mm. 95–114); and finally, a tighter, rhythmically telescoped development of the same motive (again in inversion) in the woodwinds above a tonic pedal in the timpani, which ends with a few moments of expectant waiting for the reprise (mm. 115–34). The form is rounded off by the return of the opening section, unaltered save for its final cadential portion (mm. 171–95), which is transposed down a minor third with Schubertian aplomb, all but note for note, so that it ends in C, not E♭.

In contrast to the first movement, which used harmonic tension as a source of intensity and structural force, the Scherzo is relatively relaxed harmonically; this difference is clearly encapsulated in the character – tautly wound in one and openly forthright in the other – of the motivic material of the two movements. The first chord change of the movement moves from C to D♭ (m. 7), and it is remarkable to note the simplicity with which Bruckner here moves through (by means of a direct chromatic ascent) a harmonic juncture that was so elaborately problematized in the preceding movement. Throughout the Scherzo the harmony is given to periods of triadic calmness (mm. 3–6, 33–6, 37–40, 53–64, and the corresponding spots in the second half of the movement) that are quite free of the kinetic charge that colored even the few moments of harmonic stasis in the first movement (e.g., mm. 217–24 and 369–80). So, despite its palpable rhythmic energy, the Scherzo serves as a stabilizing foil to the first movement. Here we can sense the logic of Bruckner's unusual decision to locate it before the Adagio, and to have it essay the tonic key. The Scherzo is thus able to anchor the first act of the symphony, before the long and magnificent tonal excursus enacted by the Adagio and much of the Finale.

The Trio is idiosyncratic. It is, in effect, a miniature slow movement tucked into the Scherzo. (The initial version was quite different; see Chapter 5.) The first half of the Trio has two components. The opening strain (mm. 1–24) is a touching tune that starts in A♭ major and immediately begins to drift through F minor, A♭ minor, and C♭. The contrasting section (mm. 25–44) leisurely spells out a big, brightly lit E major progression of great simplicity (four measures each of I^6, I^6_4, V^9, and I). The arrival of the root-position triad ushers in a striking moment: eight bars of pure, triadic E major stillness preceding the double bar, celebrated with rippling arpeggios played by three harps. Bruckner used harps for the first time in this symphony. He had long believed, as Friedrich Eckstein recalled, that while the harp may have been appropriate in a symphonic poem, it did not belong in "a proper symphony," but here he changed his mind. He told Eckstein that he felt compelled to use harps in this work: "I simply had to, there was no other solution."[14] The second half of the Trio begins with a brief modulatory passage (mm. 45–60) that quietly leads from E major through C major and G♭ major back to A♭ for the reprise. The opening section returns in compressed form, with a new loud passage that moves through A major (mm. 69–72), and ends with the quiet triadic dwelling at the end relocated from E major to A♭ major (mm. 85–94).

If the Scherzo looks back to the first movement, the Trio looks forward to the Adagio. Like the subsequent movement, the Trio is slow, it makes use of harps, and its primary melodic strains are intense (with many expressive appoggiaturas) and tinged by somber harmonies. In addition, it shares some harmonic elements with the slow movement, notably the tendency of major keys to melt into minor and the juxtaposition of yearning chromaticism with preternaturally still triadic music, a device that returns in the Adagio. The Trio also italicizes E major, a key that although unheard in the first movement plays a considerable role after its striking appearance in the Trio. It is the key in which the B theme of the Adagio appears, it is prominently touched upon in the powerful build-up before the climax of that movement, and it is the starting point of an oddly significant chorale-like passage that interrupts the third thematic group of the Finale.

Movement 3: *Adagio*: Feierlich langsam, doch nicht schleppend

In Romantic symphonies the two inner movements tend, as Reinhold Brinkmann wrote, to be "character pieces of 'medium' dimensions and weight . . . This is already evident in the tempo markings: Andante or Larghetto, not a large-scale Adagio; Allegretto or Moderato; not a demonic Scherzo-Allegro."[15] Bruckner is an exception to this rule, probably the greatest one: his slow movements, of which all but one are marked Adagio, are big, grand statements; his Scherzos are all boldly drawn and rhythmically charged.[16] In his slow movements Bruckner began with the Beethoven of the *Eroica* and the Ninth Symphony, not the Fifth and Sixth. The tempi are comparably slow, and the thematic principles are clearly derived: two well-characterized thematic groups, with the second group in a new key (usually some sort of mediant relation) and a brighter tempo (and occasionally a new meter), appear in alternation (thus forming expansive ABABA schemes) with, as in Beethoven's Ninth, incrementally increasing rhythmic animation. The

Table 3.1 *The formal design of the Adagio*

first cycle

	A							B			
	A1	A2	A3	A4	A1	A2	A3	B1	B2	B3	codetta
m.	1	15	18	25	29	33	36	47	67	71	81
tonality	D♭	(A⁶)	V/G♭	d♭–F	Db	(B⁶)	e♭–G	E	C	D♭	G♭→V⁷/D♭

second cycle

	A				B			
	A1	A1^{var}	A1^{var}	A4	B1	B2	B3	codetta
m.	95	109	125	134	141	161	165	169
tonality	D♭	(A⁶)	V/B♭	ab^{o7}	E♭	C♭	C	V⁹/C→V⁷/D♭

third cycle

	A								[B]
	A1	A1^{dev}	A2′	A1^{dev}	A1^{dev}	A2^{aug}	A3	A4	B1
m.	185	197	209	211	227	239	244	251	255
tonality	D♭	C♯→V⁷/B♭	A♭	E→	E→	E♭$^6_4$♭	V²/A♭	d♭–C	(D♭)

Coda

	A
	A1
m.	259–91
tonality	D♭

Adagio of the Eighth apotheosizes the genre. It carries the lyrical impulse, which can easily serve to cheer or to balm, far past the point of simple enjoyment to places of fervent vehemence. The movement's ardent expanse can feel more forbidding than enticing (it is amongst the longest and slowest slow movements in the entire symphonic repertory, challenged only by the Adagio of Bruckner's Ninth and the final movements of Mahler's Third and Ninth), but in its course it works through extreme contrasts and tensions, and by its end achieves a heroic peace.

The overall form of the Adagio is a variant of Bruckner's typical ABABA form (see Table 3.1). The movement, which inhabits an uncanny Neapolitan D♭ major, is anchored by four appearances of the opening theme, each of which begins in the tonic key only to move off in a different direction. This theme grows out of an expressively drawn melody above an accompaniment that, with its repeated chords and

Example 3.8 Adagio, mm. 15–17

indefinite, syncopated triplets, evokes the great love duet at the core of *Tristan und Isolde* ("O sink' hernieder, Nacht der Liebe").[17] (Later [at mm. 203–5] Bruckner quotes the "Siegfried" motive "in memory of the Master," as he put it.[18]) This music develops quite differently on each of its appearances. In the first statement the several thematic components, notably a great arpeggiated sixth chord (mm. 15–17, see Example 3.8), a compact chorale (mm. 18–24), and a series of plagal progressions decorated by the harps (mm. 25–8), are neatly furrowed and presented with expositional lucidity. In the second (beginning in m. 95) the striking A2 motive is entirely suppressed, and the main idea is allowed to unroll into a climactic progression. The third statement (beginning in m. 185) pushes forward rather harder, and brings back the A2 material in a moment of great drama (mm. 239–43). The final appearance of the opening material begins the coda (at m. 239), which, in marked contrast to the preceding sections, remains to luxuriate for some thirty-two measures in the tonic key.

The returns to the opening material are set off by two appearances of a relatively self-contained contrasting theme (mm. 47–80 and 141–68). This theme does not, unusually, move more quickly than does the opening theme, but it does deepen the melodic impulse of the movement. It is built around by an expressively flowing line played by the violas and cellos (see Example 3.9a).[19] In the midst of this music, a new idea emerges quite unexpectedly, only to trail off rather abruptly: the ongoing musical flux is momentarily arrested by a brief chorale sounded by the Wagner tubas (Ex. 3.9b, mm. 67–70). Within eight bars, the

Example 3.9 Adagio, second thematic group, melodic ideas
(a) mm. 47–51

(b) mm. 67–9 (brass parts only)

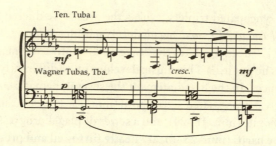

original tune loudly returns, only slightly deflected by the interrupting chorale. On its first appearance this thematic group is in the key of E major; on its return it is relocated to E♭. Just before the coda, a slight but significant fragment of the B theme appears, hovering on the threshold of the tonic (mm. 255–8).

The basic gesture of the Adagio is the movement, whether gradual or sudden, from darkness (which is described by dissonance and/or harmonic remoteness) to light, clarity, and consonance. This gesture is played out in various ways and at various levels throughout the movement, and through an increasingly elaborate *chiaroscuro* the relative values of light and dark are transfigured. In the opening theme the music circles darkly above the persistent D♭ pedal in the bass, and when the gathering dissonance is suddenly displaced by a lambent A major sixth chord in m. 15 (see Example 3.8), which is technically a pure consonance, it feels oddly unsettling. This is partly the shock of a raw triad after a long stretch of richer sonorities, and it is also due to the chord's sonic imbalance, overweighed by the thickly doubled third in the bass. The chord's special character derives also from its harmonically inexplicable appearance as an unprepared, non-functional lowered submediant. This way of making plain triads strange by locating them on distant, cross-modal relations, works even more magically in the second thematic group. The initial strain of the section feels rather dark, as much because of its use of the cello's baritone register as its E major tonality; in contrast, the tuba chorale gleams poignantly and strangely, despite its placement in a far flat-side tonality of C major. This special illumination is partly due to the replacement of the warm strings by cool brass and the unexpected instatement of a triadic, plagal progression. Here too a harmonic limit has been broached; with the chorale we have not merely reached the "darkest realm," as Kurth called it, but actually begun to emerge on the far side of the harmonic sphere.[20] In progressing from the D♭ of the Adagio's opening, to the E major that begins the second thematic group and finally coming to a C major chorale (all in the larger context of a C minor symphony) the harmonic removes become so great that the twain begin to approach each other, if not actually meet, and it is impossible to say for sure which is the light and which is the dark.

Movement 4: *Finale*: Feierlich, nicht schnell

A great deal is invested in the Finale. The first movement, potent as it is, is so tightly compressed that it does not function as the symphony's center of gravity. The Adagio may be slightly longer than the last movement (typically some 26 minutes versus about 23) and more deeply affecting, but it falls to the Finale to bring the issues raised by the whole symphony to a satisfactory conclusion. The Finale as a genre was a "problem" in the late nineteenth century symphony, and Bruckner was not free from the burden of this history.[21] He labored more over his Finales than over his other movements, and they were subject to his most radical revisions (most notably in the Third and Fourth Symphonies). It was also in his Finales that Bruckner departed most widely from formal convention, especially as regards recapitulation (see the Sixth and Seventh Symphonies). The composition of the Finale of the Eighth Symphony gave Bruckner more trouble than did the other movements, and many observers, beginning with Hermann Levi, have not found the movement wholly convincing. Bruckner did not share this opinion. The day he finished composing it, he described it as "the most significant movement of my life," and he resisted all suggestions to revise it radically.[22] It was the last Finale he was to complete, and represents a novel solution to the "Finale problem."

The formal scheme of this movement, like that of the first, is derived from sonata form, but here the thematic and tonal design is noticeably freer and ultimately follows a structural logic that is only loosely governed by what is now commonly understood as the "sonata principle," a notion that invests great importance in the structural opposition of tonic and dominant established in the exposition and then resolved in the recapitulation (see the formal outline in Table 5.1). Nor does this movement, with its almost statuesque grandeur, even feign the sense of symphonic inevitability generated by the first movement. This is not to say that the Finale does not share the musical concerns that fueled the first movement; it does, but it treats them differently. In the first movement the harmonic tensions that drove the music – which derived primarily from the C–D♭ crux – were played out vertically as much as horizontally (as in the dissonant enjambments that unsettled the reprise of the opening material). The Finale worries the opposition of C and G♭ (which is obviously derived from D♭), but does so more horizontally than vertically. In the Finale, as in the first movement, Bruckner strategically reserves decisive cadential action in the tonic key until late in the movement, and here finally the remote flat-key regions that have colored so much of the symphony are dissolved directly into the tonic key.

The movement opens very distinctively. The main theme, boldly etched, fanfare-like and played by the brass, and accompanied by an oddly hitching accompaniment pattern in the strings, begins on F♯ – which, as G♭, links retrospectively to the long stretch of D♭ that just ended the Adagio. The statement of the theme spells out a taut pattern of chromatic thirds (from F♯ to D major to B♭ minor to G♭ major before moving to D♭), and, after a repetition of this thematic unit (transposed up a major second), the music moves directly to C for the second clause of the theme, which soon secures the tonic key (mm. 31–68; note especially the cadence in mm. 38–9). Thus, unlike the unsettled opening of the first movement, this passage is clearly centripetal; it begins remotely, but moves toward the tonic. A grand pause introduces a lyrical contrast-

Example 3.10 Closing themes, Finale and first movement
(a) Finale, mm. 135–8

(b) first movement, mm. 97–100

ing thematic group (mm. 69–134) that centers on A♭ major and F minor, and includes excursions to the important flat-key reaches of C♭ (m. 99), D♭ (=C♯) minor (m. 105), and G♭ (m. 123) before closing on the dominant of E♭. The closing group of the exposition (which begins in m. 135) recalls the corresponding section of the first movement. Not only is it in the same key, E♭ minor (the "normal" contrasting key in a minor-key exposition, but not the usual mode), but in melody and texture it strongly resembles the earlier passage (see Example 3.10). This section is punctuated by a meaningful parenthesis (mm. 159–74): an austere descending line in the high violins and woodwinds high above a triadic progression in the low brass (see example 3.11) appears unannounced in the distant region of C♯ minor and creates such a sense of momentary dislocation that it seems to be a cipher or, as Kurth dubbed it, a "visionary episode."[23] It is possible to deduce some motivic antecedents of this passage (its rhythm and contour resemble ideas introduced at

Example 3.11 Finale, mm. 159–66

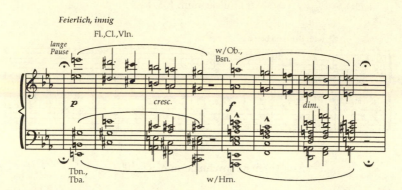

mm. 32–5 and 75–8), yet its predominant impression (because of its markedly different harmony, texture, tempo, sonority) is one of novelty.[24] This brief stretch of tranquillity suddenly vanishes behind a sustained outburst in B♭ major (mm. 183–210). The exposition ends with an expansive codetta on E♭ (mm. 215–53) that recalls the opening material and the "visionary episode" (and even hints of the Scherzo [horn, mm. 234–5]) before coming to rest on a soft timpani roll on E♭.

This exposition, while perhaps a bit diffuse, seems conventional enough in outline, if not in content. The second half of the movement is wholly unconventional; it traces an unforeseeable, yet marvelously effective, course back to the tonic key. It begins, straightforwardly enough, with a stretch of lyrical development dominated by the strings (mm. 253–300) that moves from E♭ through a poignantly songful passage in G♭ (beginning in m. 265) and culminates in an aching, chromatic progression (mm. 277–80) before ebbing in E♭ minor (mm. 285–300). The next episode is striking: it consists of a sequential series of musical units built out of the contrapuntal combination, in the brass, of prime and inverted versions of the second clause of the main theme (mm. 301–44), beginning successively on E♭ (mm. 301–8), F (mm. 323–30), and G (mm. 333–44). This G holds and is prolonged in the next section (mm. 345–86) by a very distinctive contrapuntal passage, scored with bright delicacy, that plays and replays the opening motive of the main theme, and rises by whole step until it regains G. The next section (mm. 387–436) begins, the music still lucent, with the opening theme sounding softly in the brass against a brightly lit C major figure in the violins, but soon the harmony begins to slip decisively flatwards and then pivots through D♭ on its way to a reprise of the movement's opening. This reprise begins (in m. 437) as it had in the exposition, on F♯, but now the successive statements follow a new course: B, then E, and stabilizing momentarily on A♭, before moving quickly to C (in m. 475). Thus, the tonic is regained, but only by way of a rather involved series of chromatic moves. As if to balance this circuitous approach, Bruckner follows it with a great wave of music (mm. 481–518) that rises in clear forceful steps, and then, with elemental clarity, peaks and finally descends to the dominant. Now, at last, the music articulates a cadential progression that, although it is left open, unmistakably defines C as the eventual goal (mm. 519–26).

The second thematic group now returns, but, in violation of formal convention, in the same key as in the exposition (A♭ with a pull toward F minor). The return of the contrasting theme in the tonic, or at least a key closer to the tonic, ordinarily functions as a structurally decisive stabilization. Here, things work differently. In the exposition, this thematic group did not articulate a fundamental tonal contrast; the relationship of the submediant to the tonic is markedly less polarized than is that of the dominant to the tonic and thus is in less need of resolution. Here the key of A♭ – poised between two long episodes that are strongly rooted on the dominant, G – can have the effect, as Simpson put it, "not of going away, but of coming home," yet we still await our final arrival in the tonic key.[25]

The final stage of the recapitulation begins with the return of the thematic material that had closed the exposition (mm. 583–646). This, unlike the second thematic group, is fundamentally altered upon its reappearance. It is firmly relocated to the dominant of C minor, and is initially presented in a series of loose imitative entries, beginning with an easy gait before tightening and gathering force. At the height of this process, still above G in the bass, the heavy brass intone a transformation of the theme that began the entire symphony, now in rhythmic augmentation and, more importantly, at last resolutely on the dominant and in the tonic key (compare Examples 3.12a and 3.12b). The music subsides and pauses silently above G. The coda begins calmly in C minor, and rises steadily to its famous culmination: with the full orchestra in

Example 3.12 Thematic recall in the Finale
(a) Finale, mm. 617–23 (brass parts only)

(b) first movement, mm. 23–37

brilliant fortissimo, the main themes of the four movements combine in a sonic panoply. First comes the Scherzo theme in the horns (at m. 679), along with the trumpet fanfares that punctuated the opening pages of the Finale, and as the music triumphantly reaches the tonic major in m. 697, two horns recall the sighing motive from the Adagio theme and trombones add a variant of the main theme of the first movement that is recast so as to ring a C major triad. It is, quite literally, a moment of stunning glory.

For all its splendor, this peroration avoids a decisive perfect cadence in the tonic, the archetypal symphonic gesture of hard-won victory. The dominant has, of course, been sounded at length in the second half of the movement and has dominated the sixty-odd bars preceding the coda, and yet, although the eventual arrival of the tonic is a foregone conclusion, the blaze of C major that ends the symphony (mm. 687–709) is reached through a grand plagal progression, rather than a syntactically explicit, authentic cadence (i.e., one that leads from subdominant to dominant and then tonic). Thus, the conclusive cadential preparation does not present itself as the final paroxysm of a long symphonic struggle, but rather as a self-possessed expression of splendor and at the end, the final tonic major is not wrested from the darkness with Beethovenian might, but granted to us with awesome ease. As Derek Scott aptly points out, it is exactly this sort of "unveiling" or "disclosure," that is essential to Bruckner's desire to create in his symphonies a "musical form of apocalyptic vision."[26] Bruckner's final, glorious reveling, as Robert Simpson wrote with acute poetry, "blazes with calm,"[27] yet this fire is lit not by the lamp of humanity, but, as Scott understood, by "*lux sancta*, the holy light of salvation for the believer."[28]

Programmatic levels in the Eighth Symphony

One of the central aesthetic premises of the late Romantic symphony was that instrumental music was the art best able to express or represent the barely effable Absolute, the essentially indescribable, inner essence of things. This conceptualization of musical significance, which was most influentially formulated by Schopenhauer and later Wagner, precludes – in a way that Hanslick's position that musical content comprises nothing but "tonally moving forms" does not – any simple opposition of program and absolute music. Thus, while the Eighth Symphony is in one sense undoubtedly absolute music – it engages both the musically absolute and the existential absolute – it also carries several layers of programmatic and "extramusical" significance.

First and most superficially, at its first performance in December 1892 the Symphony was accompanied by a long, unsigned program written by Josef Schalk:[29]

FIRST MOVEMENT
The figure of Aeschylus' Prometheus. – Vague, resentful defiance, with a presumptuous, titanic feeling of inner strength elevating itself above gods and fate . . . Soon the Oceanides' words of consolation . . . Terrible loneliness and silence. Soliloquy: gentle complaint rising to outbursts of delirious grief, occasionally shaken by the premonition of the bliss of redemption to come. Brazenly and unbidden the dreadful power of fate

rears up. Prometheus grindingly succumbs to the will of the hostile Cronides, and, sinking down, he cries out:

> . . . So hurl lightning's fiery snake
> down upon me, the thunderous quake of
> Wild wind's rage convulses the air . . .
> And the cruel whirlpool of Fate casts
> my body down to black Tartarus:
> Yet he cannot kill me!

SECOND MOVEMENT (SCHERZO)

The ideal elements of the first movement come forth in realistic depiction. . . . The deeds and sorrows of Prometheus appear parodic, reduced to a meager scale . . . The composer himself gave this movement the odd name "German Michael."

THE THIRD MOVEMENT (ADAGIO)

. . . the sphere of solemn, calm sublimity. Like the silent workings of divinity throned in splendor high above all earthly woe and all earthly joy . . . Not Zeus-Cronos, the inaccessible, no – the all–loving father of humanity is given to us in his entire, incalculable Grace.

> The sun resounds in age-old fashion
> With brother spheres in hymnic sound,
> And fulfills his pre-ordained round
> with thunderous progression . . .

FOURTH MOVEMENT (FINALE)

Heroism in service of the Divine. – No longer battling, suffering and succumbing solely as the bearer of his own inner strength, but as the messenger of eternal sacred Truth, herald of the idea of God . . . The work reaches its triumphant conclusion in a combination of all the main themes, from which "German Michael" is not absent; in fact, now in gleaming armor and with a swinging sword, like his namesake the Archangel, he is at the head of the flock.[30]

Schalk's program has not often found a warm reception. Reviewers of the first performance easily identified it as the work of Schalk and were content to dismiss it as banal, if not ridiculous. Hanslick and Kalbeck both mocked it, and Bruckner's supporter Carl Hruby criticized Schalk for merely providing critics with easy targets.[31] It did however exert some influence in the first decades of this century; a few commentators obviously recycled some of its motifs and several more followed Schalk in invoking Prometheus or Faust when describing the Eighth.[32] Modern critics have been content to ignore or simply forget Schalk's program; yet as Dahlhaus pointed out, many musical progressives of the later nineteenth century deemed explicative programs acceptable, even useful, as "hermeneutic 'parables,'" since although they "were considered too weak to be able to touch the 'absolute' essence of music" they could perhaps point toward it.[33] Schalk, who seems to have worked in this spirit, once compared poetic ideas to a "diver's bell" that afforded safe and rewarding immersion in the depths of the sea of music, and with his programs intended to proffer security and guidance to those trying to plumb Bruckner's symphonies.[34] However we judge the propriety of this undertaking, Schalk was quite imaginative in metaphorically mapping the form of the symphony (e.g., the soliloquy rising to "delirious grief" in the first part of the development section), and he chose his literary allusions well. His evocation of the defiance of the doomed Prometheus and of Goethe's paean to the awesome course of the Heavens do seem to point to things of importance about the symphony.

Bruckner's comments on the extramusical meanings of the symphony are now better known than is Schalk's program. The most extensive expression of them is found in a letter Bruckner wrote to Weingartner, during the conductor's ill-starred effort to perform the Eighth in early 1891:[35]

In the first movement, the trumpet and horn passage based on the rhythm of the [main] theme [mm. 369–89] is the *Todesverkündigung* [the annunciation of death], which gradually grows stronger, and finally emerges very strongly. At the end: surrender.

Scherzo: Main theme – named *deutscher Michel* [German Michael]. In the second part, the fellow wants to sleep, and in his dreamy state cannot find his tune; finally, he plaintively turns back.[36]

Finale: At the time our Emperor received the visit of the Czars at Olmütz; thus, strings: the Cossacks; brass: military music; trumpets: fanfares, as the Majesties meet. In closing, all themes; (odd), as in *Tannhäuser* in Act 2 when the King [*sic*, presumably the Landgraf] arrives; thus as *deutscher Michel* arrives from his journey, everything is already gloriously brilliant.

In the Finale there is also the death march and then (brass) transfiguration.

Bruckner's program does present a rather enigmatic face.[37] In trying to make sense of it, it might be noted that Bruckner had an ulterior motive in writing to Weingartner. By this time, he had begun to doubt gravely (and, as it turned out, correctly) that Weingartner would actually perform the symphony.[38] To some extent Bruckner may have tailored his commentary, including its incongruous association of the final thematic assemblage with the second act of *Tannhäuser* and its effort to impose a vague narrative line onto the Scherzo and the Finale, in the hope of making the symphony seem more explicitly programmatic and thus presumably more appealing to the conductor, who was a protégé of Liszt and a famous advocate of Berlioz.[39] Bruckner did not, however, dream up all of this material solely for Weingartner's benefit. He had long identified the main theme of the Scherzo with the figure "deutscher Michel," a folksy embodiment of the Teutonic that combined stout-heartedness and good-natured simplicity, and several times he stated that the opening of the Finale depicts the meeting of Emperor Franz Josef, Czar Alexander III, and Kaiser Wilhelm I of Germany at Skierniewice (not Olmütz as Bruckner thought) in September 1884.[40] Both of these associations must have had some slight political or nationalistic import at the time, but now these meanings are obscure, and in any case, such specific and relatively concrete frames of reference disarm interpretation. Indeed Schalk's program, which clearly betrays knowledge of Bruckner's comments, seems in part an attempt to flesh them out and translate them into a form that is at once more conventional and less precise, and thus more amenable to concert-hall, and indeed coffee-house, exegesis.

Bruckner's explanation of the eschatological symbolism of the climax and conclusion of the first movement is undoubtedly of greater hermeneutic value. Not only did Bruckner refer to it on several occasions, but his various comments on it are consistent, they offer richer soil for individual interpretation, and, most importantly, they make palpable musical sense: the last part of the first movement is striking, both in form and content, and it is not hard to accept that there is something extramusical at play here. Bruckner described the coda as a grim scene: "this is how it is when one is on his deathbed, and opposite hangs a clock, which, while his life comes to its end, beats on ever steadily: tick, tock, tick, tock," a scenario that nicely captures the ominous severity of the music.[41] Bruckner's identification of the massive horn call that precedes the coda as the *Todesverkündigung* is similarly apt. This moment in the symphony does sound terribly portentous; moreover, Bruckner's label inevitably recalls the fourth scene in the second act of *Die Walküre*, which is commonly known by the same name. Although this part of the symphony sounds nothing like the scene in Wagner's opera, Bruckner's verbal allusion to it opens onto programmatic connotations that recall Schalk's: Siegmund's extreme devotion to Sieglinde and Brünnhilde's disobedient mercy both contain a seed of Promethean rebellion.

In the end, however, Bruckner's, and for that matter Schalk's, extramusical comments are curiously unsatisfying. Perhaps they are best seen not as interpretive keys, but as reflections of what Korte called the *Doppeldasein*, the double existence, of the Eighth Symphony.[42] The work unites an expressive intensity, which seems to encode metaphysical meanings, and an intense musicality, which resists any concrete explanation. The motivic recurrences and transformations that cut across the symphony and the scattered thematic allusions, especially Wagnerian ones (notably the evocation of Tristan and Isolde's love music in the main theme of the Adagio and the sounding of the Siegfried motive later in that movement [horns, mm. 203–5]), that flicker across it carry a charge of palpable, if unconsummated, associative meaning.[43] In some passages the music reaches such an uncommon depth of expression that it seems to give sounding form to intense subjective experiences, whether through sheer physical impact (as at the moment of reprise in the first movement, the grandiose perorations in the first and third movements, or the beginning of the Finale) or through extraordinary lyrical fervor (in several stretches of the Adagio). Furthermore, some phases of the symphony's unfolding respond to expressive ends, not formal convention: the unusual recapitulation in the first movement, especially its precipitant treatment of the third thematic group; the great climactic deflection before the coda of the Adagio; the oddly intrusive "visionary episode" in the Finale exposition; and the dramatic recasting of the third group in the recapitulation into a great *Steigerung* that culminates in a transformed reminiscence of the thematic gesture that opened the symphony.[44] In pushing so urgently, and so meaningfully, at the stylistic limits of symphonic expression, these passages foreclose the possibility that this symphony is a pure agon of "tonally moving forms" and insist that we accept it as an affair of considerable symbolic depth.

4

The Adagio and the sublime

Allusions to sublimity often color descriptions of Bruckner's music.
Program notes and serious criticism alike have long effused about the
transcendent, metaphysical depth of the symphonies, and the Adagio of
the Eighth Symphony has been identified as "sublime" with particular
frequency. Josef Schalk's program identified the Adagio as a "sphere of
calm, solemn sublimity," and ever since, the term "sublime" has been
prone to attach itself to this movement.[1] A popular guide to Bruckner's
symphonies published in 1907 called this Adagio "one of the most sol-
emnly transfigurative, splendid, and sublime tone-pieces ever written."[2]
Bruckner's first American biographer, Gabriel Engel, referred to it as
"the sublime slow movement . . . [that] rises to unprecedented heights of
devotional ecstasy."[3] As recently as 1997 Edward Rothstein placed the
Eighth on a short list of works that successfully aspire to sublimity.[4]

The tradition of linking Bruckner's symphonies with transcendent
sublimity derives from various sources. It reflects the common awareness of Bruckner's religiosity as a person, as a church musician, and as a
composer of both sacred music and symphonies. The genre of the symphony itself has long been associated with the sublime. Sulzer's *Allgemeine Theorie der schönen Künste* (1792) identified the symphonic Allegro
as a genre "admirably suited to the expression of grandeur, of the festive
and sublime."[5] Some eighty years later, Wagner declared in his centenary
essay *Beethoven* that "the only aesthetic term to use" to describe the
effect of Beethoven's Seventh and Eighth Symphonies is "the *Sublime*."[6]
Modern critics have continued to connect the symphony and the
sublime; recently, Reinhold Brinkmann stated simply that "the theory of
the symphony was always related to the aesthetics of the sublime."[7] In
late nineteenth-century practice, slow movements, with their intimations of the otherworldly and their temporal expansion, increasingly

came to carry the main weight of the desire to find in the symphony expressions of the most profound and spiritual kind, and Bruckner, who was sometimes styled as the great "Adagio–Komponist," was perceived as the greatest exponent of the ideal of the symphony as sublimely symbolic.[8]

We may be conditioned, therefore, to associate Bruckner's symphonies with sublimity casually, even reflexively; indeed, the term "sublime" has itself something of a dual character. While it is often used quite loosely to denote something outstanding, impressive, or awesome, in philosophy and aesthetics – from Shaftesbury through Kant to Lyotard – the concept of the sublime has acquired a fairly specific range of significance and, as we shall see, it was often an important category in nineteenth-century aesthetics. Bruckner critics may not have always worked with full cognizance of this tradition, yet approaching Bruckner's music from the vantage of the aesthetics of the sublime can reveal aspects of both its musical substance and its cultural meaning. This chapter thus has three tasks: to sketch out the idea of the sublime and capture something of its historical and conceptual density; to consider how the Adagio of Bruckner's Eighth Symphony stages itself as sublime; and, finally, to explore how this musical sublimity might have resonated in the Vienna of his time.

The sublime aesthetic

The history of the sublime as an aesthetic category begins with a treatise entitled *On the Sublime* (*Peri Hypsous*) by Longinus, a Greek writer active in the first century AD. [9] Longinus' goal was to show, through both explanation and demonstration, how rhetoric could express grand and elevated ideas and exercise the passions to the level of "intense and enthusiastic emotion."[10] Longinus' work was also important in that it codified qualities that were to remain central to later notions of the sublime: seriousness, grandeur, depth of meaning and feeling, passion, enthusiasm even to the level of violence. Although it is essentially an essay on rhetoric (with chapters on figures, oaths, similes, periphrasis, and so forth), *On the Sublime* is oddly reticent to define the sublime as strictly a rhetorical manner. For example, Longinus' statement that sublimity is "the resonance of a great mind," carefully leaves open some doubt whether the mind in question is that of the persuasive speaker or that of the listener who is raised to ecstasy.[11] This ambiguity is inherent in "true sublimity," which as Longinus put it, fills one "with delight and great glory, as if our soul itself had created what it had just heard."[12] Longinus' work thus contains a productive tension between author, text, and audience that was to inform many of the richest and most interesting subsequent discussions of the sublime.

Despite its venerable origins, the idea of the sublime, with its preference for the passionately expressive rather than the serenely beautiful, exerted only modest influence until the eighteenth century.[13] As David Simpson wrote, "those generations for whom some model of decorum was the presiding ethic tended to consign whatever seemed excessive or irregular to the realm of the grotesque or bizarre, rather than to a positively validated sublime."[14] Even in the eighteenth century, when the sublime began to attract serious attention, the classical sense of the term as a rhetorical mode or a manner of address tended to hold. This was clearly true in music. During this era, the musical sublime was conceived of within the prevailing system of musical rhetoric; it was identified with the elevated, the serious, the grave and impressive.[15] Concern was focused less on the affective response of the individual listener than on a composer's deployment of a common stock of stylistic signs and *topoi*.[16]

In the decades before 1800, with the first stirrings of Romanticism, sublimity became a focus of renewed critical interest.[17] Edmund Burke's *A Philosophical Enquiry into the Origin of our Ideas of the Sublime and The Beautiful* of 1757 was the watershed of an emerging revaluation of the sublime.[18] Burke was concerned to expand the domain of aesthetic value beyond beauty and find a place for more intense, and less immediately appealing, realms of experience. He set up a basic opposition between two aesthetic categories, the beautiful and the sublime. Beauty is charming and pleasing; it is that which arouses delight and "love," which Burke identified as "satisfaction" unclouded by "desire or lust."[19] Sublimity is quite opposite; it arises not from satisfaction or contentment, but from strong, often dark emotions: fear, terror, and dread. As Burke wrote, "Whatever is fitted in any sort to excite the ideas of pain, and danger, that is to say, whatever is in any sort terrible, or is conversant about terrible objects . . . is a source of the sublime."[20] In a well-known passage, Burke contrasted the physical traits of beautiful and sublime objects: he characterized those beautiful as small, smooth, polished, light and delicate, and those sublime as vast, great, rugged, negligent, gloomy, dark, and massive.

Although it was not his main concern, Burke did begin to gauge the psychological aspects of sublimity. He speculated on why sublime objects should induce in us an astonishment verging on horror, and concluded that this response was born of our inability adequately to perceive grand and confusing objects. This epistemological dimension of the sublime – its straining at the limits of our powers of "apprehensive synthesis" – was to become the basis of the most important nineteenth-century understandings of the concept.[21] The crucial moves in the Romantic appropriation of the sublime were made by Immanuel Kant in his *Critique of Judgment* (1790). Kant emphasized that sublimity is not a quality objectively inherent in things, whether natural or man-made, but is instead a mental state arising from our apprehension of them. When we are confronted by an object that is "great beyond all standards of sense," he wrote, "it makes us judge as *sublime*, not so much the object, as our own state of mind in the estimation of it."[22] Kant's aesthetics argue that the intuition of sublimity arises from the failure of our empirical faculties: when our senses prove incapable of comprehending an object as a coherent totality, we become "aware, by contrast, of the magnificence of Reason itself. The resulting feeling is the feeling of the sublime."[23] Paradoxically, it is only because of the frustration of our power to perceive external reality that we are able, indeed compelled, to realize the superiority of what Kant called Reason, our innately transcendent rational and moral dimensions. This is "the importance of the sublime," Thomas Weiskel wrote in his extraordinary *The Romantic Sublime*, it "is the very moment in which the mind turns within and performs its identification with reason."[24] This identification thereby "resolves the traumatic disequilibrium of the sublime moment [through] a metaphorical substitution of a 'power within' for the external power. The power within, Kant tells us, is greater far than the external power – to which, however, we remain subject as natural beings."[25]

By the beginning of the nineteenth century the sublime had become a basic component in Romantic aesthetics. The Romantic sublime grew out of Kant's understanding of sublimity as revelatory experience, and in contrast to eighteenth-century versions, the nineteenth-century sublime emphasized the subjective component of sublimity and its intensely inward process of subsuming "the perceiving mind into the eternal and infinite."[26] In music, then, expressions of sublimity along with other means of musical signification began to migrate, as Richard Taruskin put it, from such public, "socially sanctioned" codes as genre, rhetoric, and the doctrine of the affections to the "gnomic, hermetic" modes of expression that characterized absolute music in the age of Beethoven, Schopenhauer, and Wagner.[27] Around the turn of the nineteenth century, we can see the emergence of this new understanding of the musical sublime. Critics continued to identify certain styles and musical manners – typically grand and serious ones – as sublime; at the same time, Kant's notion of sublimity as a moment of "epistemological transcendence" began to infiltrate discourses on music. Both tendencies can be found in William Crotch's lectures on music (which originated as early as 1800). His definition baldly juxtaposes a Kantian sensibility with a more traditional rhetorical sense: "The sublime is founded on principles of vastness and incomprehensibility. The word sublime originally signifies high, lofty, elevated; and this style accordingly never descends to anything small delicate, light, pretty, playful or comic. The grandest style is therefore the sacred style – that of the church and oratorio . . . where the words express the most awful and striking images."[28]

In 1805 the German aesthetician Christian Friedrich Michaelis published "On the Beautiful and Sublime in Music," which was perhaps the earliest thoroughgoing attempt to work out the musical implications of Kant's model of sublime transcendence.[29] "The feeling of sublimity in music," he wrote, "is aroused when the imagination is elevated to the plane of the limitless, the immeasurable, the unconquerable. This happens when such emotions are aroused as either completely prevent the integration of one's impressions into a coherent whole, or when at any rate they make it very difficult." Michaelis argued that this difficulty could derive from two distinct types of musical phenomenon: from entrancing uniformity and repetition or from musical diversity and complexity so great as to dazzle the ear. "Thus," he concluded, "in music, the sublime can only be that which seems too vast and significant, too strange and wonderful, to be easily assimilated . . . Sublime notes, figuration and harmonies stimulate the imagination, which must exert itself and expand beyond its normal bounds to grasp, integrate and recall them." It is this musical sublime of surpassing strangeness and complexity that is engaged by Bruckner's symphonies.

Articulations of sublimity in the Adagio

Kant identified two genres of sublimity, the dynamical sublime and the mathematical sublime. The dynamical sublime, the more straightforward and traditional of the two, is the sense of awe inspired by objects that seem to have power over us. It is akin to (and was, in fact, influenced by) Burke's notion that the sublime is always a "modification of power" and as a rule involves fright and terror.[30] The Adagio of the Eighth Symphony explicitly plays at the dynamical sublime, with the frightening vehemence of its great climaxes, and its sheer sonic force. Indeed, Burke's adjectives seem tailor-made: great, rugged, negligent, gloomy, dark, and massive.

Less obvious but ultimately more meaningful are the ways in which the Adagio engages Kant's other category, the mathematical sublime. The mathematical sublime arises from that "which would force us to push . . . comprehension . . . to the bounds of the faculty of imagination," whether by means of sheer size and expansiveness (Kant's famous example is the Pyramids of Egypt) or by aesthetic complexity.[31] Here, again, Bruckner symphonies, with their expansiveness and, especially, their distinctive synthesis of formal convention and novel execution, quite obviously engage the mathematical sublime. Franz Schalk detected this early on: "Bruckner's forms were so simple, so direct, that at first people overlooked them, as if they were not there. People wailed about chaotic incoherence, about pointless climaxes, about illogic and willfulness. As people finally began to comprehend Bruckner's works as wholes, suddenly they stood clear in their primitive symmetry. They were the old classic symphonic forms, but built up into tremendous, sublime monumentality, in dimensions that no one could grasp up close."[32] Here we have something very much like Kant's Pyramids.

The Adagio works at mathematical sublimity in another way, too, which lies a bit deeper and by its very nature challenges comprehension. Throughout the movement, Bruckner deploys a series of increasingly extreme harmonic progressions; these seem designed to astonish the ear,

Example 4.1 Adagio, mm. 1–20, harmonic reduction

to push it past its normal habitus, and ultimately set in motion the process of sublime crisis and sudden revelation. These passages move at the limits of the harmonic vocabulary of the late nineteenth century, the realm of enharmonic equivalence and symmetrical pitch formations – the sorts of things that, as Richard Cohn recently wrote, are capable of "inducing a mild type of vertigo,"[33] or as Bruckner's pupil Friedrich Eckstein put it, reveal "new, almost incomprehensible musical wonders" and "mysteries of daring chromaticism and enharmonicism."[34]

The Adagio is in the key of D♭, and as we have seen, the first movement makes considerable use of D♭ (motivically, more than tonally), but it is little heard in the Scherzo so that at its onset the tonality of the Adagio sounds fresh, even a bit precarious, yet not wholly new. (Bruckner's late decision to place the Adagio after the Scherzo was likely inspired in part by considerations of key scheme; see Chapter 5.) The movement opens with a broad thematic statement (mm. 1–20) that unfolds above an unmoving tonic pedal, harmonized initially with a D♭ major triad and at the end by a dominant seventh on D♭ (see Example 4.1). What is remarkable is how D♭ is treated in the middle of the passage. Bruckner overlays the tonic pedal with an array of chromatic, often dissonant harmonies that inflect the tonic enharmonically. The major key almost immediately begins to shade into the parallel minor (mm. 4–5), and beginning with the second phrase (mm. 7–10), D♭ is treated as C♯, if in a rather enigmatic way. The harmony slides toward F♯ minor, producing a dominant sonority, which emphasizes D♮, a pitch that contravenes the tonic status of D♭. Still above the D♭/C♯ in the bass, the music rises to an oddly massive A major sixth chord (mm. 15–17), which is marked by a wide, sweeping arpeggio figure, crowned by a distinctive turn figure (see Example 3.8). Then, with no further ado, there is a quick enharmonic move back to D♭, where the passage comes to rest. This harmonic display serves no direct structural function: it does not tonicize a new tonal area, nor does it even solidly define the tonic key. Rather it sits sphinx-like at the portal of the movement, and adumbrates a tendency to harmonic quixotism that characterizes several later junctures of the movement. The movement is shaped by a series of odd and unforeseen tonal slips that hinge on enharmonic progressions. The most important of these utilize the gesture of mm. 15–17, which, it is worth noting, is immediately marked off, as it were, by its appearance in a distinctive tonal region (A major, the lowered submediant major) and an eccentric harmonic setting (a major triad in first inversion, with the third massively doubled[35]).

The movement is tripartite. Each section begins by restating the opening material and then cycles through the basic thematic material, although in slightly different ways each time (see Table 3.1). The final section (mm. 185–258) brings the harmonic processes of the movement to a culmination. It starts with the music that opened the movement, and, for the first time, the enharmonic potential of D♭ to function as C♯ (and lead to D) is unleashed (m. 193). This freeing of harmonic energy sets in motion a series of tonal waves (to borrow Ernst Kurth's terminology) that rise chromatically and crest over irregular cadential progressions. The first of these waves (mm. 185–210) rises above a series of ascending half steps in the bass from D♭ (=C♯) to E and, after a short digression, F, which serves briefly as the basis for a forceful dominant preparation in B♭ minor (mm. 205–7; see Example 4.2). At its height, this dominant collection shades into a half-diminished chord, which in turn functions as a pre-dominant in A♭ and progresses to a massive statement of the arpeggio motive from mm. 15–16 on a 6/4 chord in A♭ (mm. 208–10). Just as this gesture is reaching for a conventional resolution, via its dominant seventh, the ground slips out from under it and the music is suddenly becalmed on E major, whereupon another wave begins to stir.

This second wave (mm. 211–26) is more intense and strongly

Example 4.2 Adagio, mm. 204–11, harmonic reduction

Example 4.3 Adagio, mm. 214–27, reduction

directed. It rises through a long series of chromatically ascending parallel tenths (see Example 4.3). As the volume of sound grows, the music builds and begins to compress and tighten, and the wave peaks through a quick series of seventh chords and culminates in a great dissonant knot that collapses the difference between dominant seventh and augmented sixth (m. 225, note the play between F/F♭ and G/G♭). At this pinnacle, the music simply stops. After a moment of silence, the movement resumes quietly, again on E major. For a second time, an intensifying wave has suddenly ebbed, its power dissipated by an irregular, enharmonic progression, to mystifyingly inconclusive effect.

The third and final wave (mm. 227–38) again builds on an ascending bass (see Example 4.4). It quickly arrives at a grandiose peroration in C♭, with a series of uncanny parallel sixth chords in the brass, and moves with great power through a searing 4/2 chord (mm. 237–8), crowned with a flurry of trumpet calls as the basses and cellos strain at the top of their

Example 4.4 Adagio, mm. 227–47, reduction

Example 4.5 Adagio, coda (harmonic reduction)

range. Now, at last, a wave breaks with full force: the dissonance discharges itself enharmonically onto a huge, bald E♭ major 6/4 chord, which is topped by a crash from the cymbal and triangle, harp arpeggios, and an announcement of the arpeggio theme in augmentation (mm. 239–42). This almost absurd magnification of the most basic of cadential gestures tries with all of its might to prepare us for an authentic cadence. It is not to be. Just as the dominant of E♭ is driving to close on its tonic, we are thrown back, crushingly, to C♭ (mm. 242–3). With a huge shift of register, the music quickly comes to rest on the dominant of A♭, and the force of the wave dissipates through a series of plagal progressions before finally drifting to a halt on C. From this uncertain point in harmonic space, the music cadences with disarming simplicity in the tonic, D♭ (see Example 4.5). The ensuing coda is a mirror image of the opening pages of the movement. It is based on a long, unmoving tonic pedal, but the coda – in marked contrast to the opening – luxuriates in the tonic key. The music unfurls a peaceful, secure tonality. The stress and angst of the preceding episodes are wholly, almost miraculously, absent.

The Adagio – with its staggering climaxes, its dazzling harmonic shifts, its mysteriously fractured form, and its abrupt juxtapositions of violent upheaval and uncanny stillness – plays out a sublime plot. Bruckner's willfully esoteric tonal schemes eschew conventional means of expressing harmonic coherence. The stunning collapses that fissure the last third of the movement strain heroically at the limits of symphonic possibility, and physically enact what Schopenhauer called the "conscious and violent tearing away" that epitomizes the moment of sublime crisis.[36] Finally, with the arrival of the remarkably still coda, which by some standards might be judged inadequately motivated or artificially easy, we are presented with a sonic expression of Kant's model of sublime satisfaction: faced with music that "bewilders" and "perplexes" our power of apprehension, the "imagination, in striving to surpass [its maximum], sinks back into itself, by which, however, a kind of emotional satisfaction is produced."[37] If, as Raimonda Modiano wrote, Kant's sublime is a fantasy in which the mind "suspends disbelief for a moment; it pretends to itself that nature is sublime in order to claim sublimity for itself and savor its power over nature," then the unforeseen *lieto fine* of the coda is the key to the parable of sublimity portrayed in the Adagio.[38] For much of its length, the Adagio seems insuperably complex; but in a passage of sublime transcendence, this perception is unmasked as a fiction by the miraculous resolution of the coda, which ecstatically dissolves everything into D♭ major serenity.

The meaning of sublimity in Bruckner's Vienna

Bruckner's music provoked the ire of many of his early Viennese listeners, and this outrage was clearly recorded by a group of critics headed by Hanslick, who responded to Bruckner with high levels of distaste, invective, and even fear. A classic formulation of the case against Bruckner is found in Hanslick's review of the premiere of the Eighth Symphony (which was already quoted in Chapter 1).[39] Although he did not use the term, Hanslick focused with remarkable acuity on exactly those musical traits that Bruckner used to articulate sublimity, namely expansiveness, harmonic complexity, stunning power and repetition. "Characteristic of Bruckner's newest C minor symphony," he wrote, "is the immediate juxtaposition of dry, contrapuntal academicism with unrestrained exultation. Thus tossed between drunkenness and desolation, we achieve. . . no artistic contentment . . ." Hanslick specifically criticized Bruckner's way of building climaxes: he "begins with a short chromatic motive, repeats it over and over again, higher and higher in the scale and on into infinity, augments it, diminishes it, offers it in contrary motion, and so on, until the listener is simply crushed under the sheer weight and monotony of this interminable lamentation." Hanslick even described the effect of being sublimely overwhelmed, although without achieving the transport of "epistemological transcendence" that is the essence of the sublime experience; as he described it, he was "tossed between intoxication and desolation," but in the end was left "simply crushed," not inspired or moved to ecstasy.

We might dismiss Hanslick as simply insensible to musical transport and write off his critique as reactionary carping. Yet taken in its social and political context, Hanslick's rejection of Bruckner's aspirations to sublimity makes sense. Bruckner's music tended to appeal most strongly to people, typically younger ones, who, under the star of Wagner and Nietzsche, felt alienated by what they saw as the lifeless culture of the Viennese establishment. Hanslick, like most of Bruckner's committed opponents, represented social institutions (the University, the *Neue Freie Presse*, and, by extension, the professional and bureaucratic classes) that were pillars of the bourgeois order that had come to control the Viennese polity in the 1860s and 1870s.[40] At the time, the links between the social, the political and the musical were keenly felt. In 1896 Heinrich Schuster wrote, for example, that "the opposition to Bruckner was and is a factional matter, and in fact, it emanates from the party that means the same thing in the field of music that the old liberal does in the field of politics."[41] Audience reactions to Bruckner's music did reflect social divisions. After a performance of the Third Symphony at a subscription concert of the Vienna Philharmonic in 1891, one critic reported that the galleries, which contained the only seats accessible to Bruckner's young partisans, "rang out with noisy demonstrative applause." In contrast, the parquet, which was occupied by old-guard subscribers, "began to empty after the first movement, and this process was repeated in increasing measure after each subsequent movement."[42]

Hanslick's abjuration of Bruckner's sublime had a certain aesthetic logic as well. Hanslick's commitment to what he called "the musically beautiful" epitomizes the position of those who rejected Bruckner on principle. For Hanslick, "the primordial stuff of music is regular and pleasing sound," which should operate "logically" on the mind; this is hardly the stuff of sublimity. In fact, the musical sublime, which depends on inducing states of emotional intensity in the listener, found no welcome place in Hanslick's scheme. He frankly distrusted as "pathological" music and musical responses that were primarily concerned with the arousal of passions and emotions.[43]

Hanslick's musical ideal, its valorization of logic, internal coherence, and sober satisfaction, can be interpreted as a musical embodiment of what Max Weber was later to call "rationalization," the principle of basing social organization and action on the practical application of reason – rather than on custom or tradition – in pursuit of efficiency, utility, and control. Rationalization was a crucial component of Weber's "spirit of capitalism" and the Viennese Liberal sphere, which Hanslick so successfully inhabited, was an early instantiation of rational, materialist, bureaucratic modernity.[44] Bruckner's symphonies sounded a different ethos – one drawing on Catholic piety, charismatic populism, Wagnerism, and atavistic mysticism – and thus mobilized opposing musical, cognitive, and, ultimately, social impulses. Sublimity, with its dialectical overcoming of empirical objectivity, is inimical to Apollonian order and the sovereignty of worldly rationality, to name two impulses that were at the heart of the ideology of Viennese Liberalism.

The sublime has always been fraught with revolutionary implications.[45] Radicals often embraced its possibility of tearing away the veil of convention. Others recoiled from the sublime as a force that could sunder the proper, traditional order of things. The sublime was politicized, for example, by Burke in his classic counter-revolutionary statement, *Reflections on the Revolution in France* (1790). Burke vehemently rejected the French Revolution and its goal of reconstructing society around a set of abstract ideas (namely *fraternité*, *égalité*, *liberté*) as an illegitimate violation of the historically established social order, which, Burke believed, was a reflection of natural and divine laws. As several scholars, notably William R. Musgrave, have recently argued, Burke's political ideas and his aesthetic ideas link up. For Burke, the monstrousness of the revolution resided in its freeing of the "threat of sublime energy to dislocate itself from these customary institutional constraints – to produce a self-authorizing political agent."[46] Although it is not possible directly to transpose Burke's attitude to fin-de-siècle Vienna, intimations of the revolutionary moment inherent in sublimity may help explain the extraordinary defensiveness expressed by Bruckner's antagonists. Gustav Dömpke, a critic closely allied to Hanslick, did in fact denounce Bruckner in terms that not only were explicitly political but actually invoked the threat of palace revolution. Bruckner, he wrote, "composes nothing but high treason, rebellion and regicide. [He] is by far the most dangerous of the musical innovators of the day."[47] Yet to others, who held different cultural and political ideals, the "sublime energy" unleashed by Bruckner's music was a welcome force. At a Bruckner concert given by the Vienna Philharmonic in 1888, a young Hugo Wolf jumped up and shouted while "menacingly and imperiously raising his fist: 'Attention! Now the sublimest part is starting,'" and, as Max Graf later reported, "it sounded like a battle cry."[48]

5

The 1887 version and the 1890 version

The 1887 version of the Eighth Symphony has had a rather odd career. In the aftermath of Hermann Levi's negative appraisal in the fall of 1887, Bruckner set it aside, and it was soon eclipsed by the revised version of 1890. It was not until the appearance of Nowak's modern edition in 1972 that the score became available for study, performance and, inevitably, comparison against the canonical 1890 version. For several decades before this, however, the 1887 version, then known only by reputation, and the events surrounding its revision led a shadow existence. During the "Bruckner-Streit" of the mid-1930s – the debate in Germany and Austria about the authenticity of the previously available editions of Bruckner's works sparked by the appearance and promulgation of the initial volumes of Robert Haas's collected edition – Levi's reaction to the first version of the symphony occasioned far-reaching interpretation and speculation, some of it extravagant. For example, Haas asserted, without offering substantiation, that it depressed Bruckner to the point that he entertained "suicidal notions [*Selbstmordgrillen*]."[1] A number of writers and scholars, including Haas, came to believe that the incident and its psychological after-effects were decisive in sending Bruckner into what they saw as a spiral of uncertainty and self-doubt, during which he undertook, at least partly at external behest, a series of ill-advised revisions of not only the Eighth Symphony, but also the First, Third, and Fourth Symphonies (all of which were revised between 1887 and 1890).[2] It was argued that because of their ostensibly compromised origins, the revised versions of these works were less than fully authentic and needed to be discarded in favor of new editions based on Bruckner's "pure" manuscript scores. Several of Haas's later editions (notably the Fourth Symphony [1936], the Second Symphony [1938] and the Seventh Symphony [1944]) put this belief into practice, and in his edition of the Eighth Symphony (1939) Haas went so far as to incorporate passages of the 1887 version into the 1890 version in an effort to construct an "ideal" text that, as he put it, restored the work's "organic life-essentials," which had supposedly been compromised by external pressure during the revision (see Appendix A).[3] Several influential Brucknerians, notably Robert Simpson and Deryck Cooke, subsequently championed Haas's skepticism about the authorship of the 1890 version. Cooke, who asserted that Bruckner was beset by a "deep sense of insecurity in the face of others' criticism," believed that Josef Schalk exerted substantial, direct influence on the 1890 version, which he labeled dismissively as the "Bruckner–Schalk revision."[4]

These doubts about the authenticity of the 1890 revision are misplaced. They stem ultimately from a highly questionable, albeit traditional, view of Bruckner as a naive genius beset by his circumstances and prone to unwise compromise. In the 1930s, as Haas's revisionist arguments against the authenticity of the late, revised versions of Bruckner's symphonies began to circulate, several of the composer's surviving acquaintances rejected any suggestion that the composer was liable to manipulation or even that he was open to persuasion.[5] Josef V. von Wöss (1863–1943) denied that the revision of the Eighth was compromised in this way and offered a reminiscence of Bruckner's steadfastness in the face of unwanted editorial advice: "at a gathering at [the Gasthaus] Gause at the time of the revision of the Eighth, Bruckner took out a page, pointed out to the students a passage for wind instruments and said: 'I have simply scored it this way, and if you rascals [*Viechkerln*] keep arguing with me . . . ,' at that he angrily raised his clenched fist like Zeus hurling lightning bolts."[6] More importantly, as Leopold Nowak bluntly emphasized, "all of the corrections in the autograph [score of the 1890 version] stem from Bruckner and there is no sign of other handwriting."[7] Nowak sensibly – and rightly – supplanted Haas's edition with a modern edition of the 1890 version (1955), which he later supplemented with an edition of the 1887 version. As Nowak recognized, the 1887 version and the 1890 version are exactly that: self-standing, complete *versions* of the same symphony. In the later version the orchestration was revamped somewhat, a few passages recomposed, and some short passages simply deleted, especially in the Finale. Bruckner himself regarded these revisions as "improvements [*Verbesserungen*]" and clearly felt that the 1890 version superseded the earlier one.[8] Yet the 1887 version is not only undoubtedly legitimate, but it has an integrity and musical logic of its own. It also opens a fascinating series of perspectives on the 1890 version, Bruckner's approach to revision, and his evolving view of the symphony.

The nature of the 1890 revision

While it is obvious that Levi's opinion that the first version was deeply flawed was the spur that prompted Bruckner to rework the piece, Levi's influence on the revised version can easily be overestimated. Any suggestion that Bruckner either slavishly submitted to his opinion or revised the piece in a state of emotional collapse is surely mistaken. Bruckner was, naturally, taken aback and deeply dismayed by the negative response of his trusted colleague, yet he rebounded in a reasonable time and was never thrown into profound despair (see Chapter 2). The composer realized that Levi had reason to cavil at some aspects of the symphony (notably the orchestration), but he also had the sureness of vision to see that the conductor's overall response reflected an inability to grasp the work as a whole. Indeed, if nothing else, Levi's reaction demonstrated dramatically that in its initial version, the work failed to make itself understood to someone who, as a consummate conductor of the most advanced music, certainly should have been able to fathom it. With his critical judgment thus piqued Bruckner returned to the symphony. The musical substance of Bruckner's revision, which as we shall see goes far beyond simple adjustments and refinements, shows that he neither merely capitulated to Levi's judgment (let alone Schalk's) nor attempted to mollify or simplify his initial conception; rather, he sharpened his conception of the symphony.

Revisions to the orchestration

Levi stated frankly that he considered Bruckner's use of the orchestra, particularly "the trumpets and tubas (really of the winds in general)," to be "impossible."[9] In his revision Bruckner did not generally simplify his orchestration; indeed he actually enlarged the woodwind choir by calling for triple woodwinds in all four movements, not only the Finale as in the 1887 version. He did, however, heed Levi's concern about his usage of the

Wagner tubas. The inclusion of a quartet of Wagner tubas in a symphony was highly unusual; Bruckner's Seventh had been the first symphony to include these instruments, which were famously introduced in *Der Ring des Nibelungen*.[10] In the Seventh these instruments are confined to the Adagio and the Finale, reserved for passages where their distinctive sonority is important, not given rhythmically active parts, nor used for very long stretches. The tuba quartet is, in effect, used as an adjunct to the regular orchestral forces. A clear example is the coda of the Adagio, where the four Wagner tubas provide a striking timbral accompaniment to the horns. (This is similar to Wagner's prominent use of these instruments as a means of casting a somber hue across the music, e.g., Hunding's music [*Die Walküre*, Act 1], the *Todesverkündigung* scene [*Die Walküre*, Act 2, scene 4], and Siegfried's death [*Götterdämmerung*, Act 3, scene 2].)

In the Eighth Symphony Bruckner used the Wagner tubas more extensively. He included them in every movement but the Scherzo. In the Adagio and Finale they are handled much as they were in the Seventh, but in the 1887 first movement they are used with considerably more freedom: the opening thematic statement includes two exposed interjections by them (mm. 27–8 and 31–2); they are featured in the harmonically intense opening of the development section (mm. 157–93); and they are used liberally throughout the movement, especially in heavily scored sections (e.g., mm. 102–43 and 425–53). While these tuba parts may not quite be "impossible" (as recent recordings demonstrate), it is understandable that Levi found them unidiomatic and needlessly difficult. Bruckner himself seems to have sensed quite early on that his use of the Wagner tubas in the first movement was immoderate; even in the 1887 version he deployed them far more judiciously in the Adagio and Finale, both of which were orchestrated after the first movement and both of which require eight horn players with four doubling on Wagner tuba. And in the 1890 version Bruckner notably scaled back his use of the Wagner tubas in the first movement, too. Instead of scoring the movement for four horns and four Wagner tubas as he had in 1887, he used eight horn players, four doubling on tubas; in this way Bruckner was able to reserve the Wagner tubas for those places where their special timbre was used to effect (e.g., the first part of the development section) without having to press them into service where horns were better suited (e.g., most big tuttis).

Bruckner's revisions to the orchestration, aside from the Wagner tubas, stem less from Levi's influence than the composer's growing mastery of orchestral ends and means (it is worth recalling he had prepared the final versions of the Fourth [1887–8] and Third Symphonies [1888–9], both of which incorporate orchestral modifications, in the interim). Most of these changes move in the direction of greater clarity and directness, but not always by simplification. The scoring of some of the passages for full orchestra is slightly less busy and cluttered in the 1890 version (compare the woodwinds in mm. 559–70 of the Finale in the 1887 version and mm. 527–34 of the 1890 version), while others are made more massively imposing (compare mm. 225–32 of the first movement in the 1887 version and mm. 217–24 of the 1890 version). Some of the reorchestration in the 1890 version reflects a subtly different compositional conception. Consider the differing scoring of the loud restatement of the opening theme of the first movement (mm. 23–44 in both versions): in 1887, the theme is immediately sounded in a three-octave unison by trumpets, trombone, bass tuba, and low strings; in the 1890 version the trombones are replaced by the horns and the trumpets play not the actual theme, but instead only its bare rhythm. These changes do lessen the simple power of the 1887 scoring, but they do have two longer-range effects. The withholding of the full weight of the combined horns, trumpets, and trombones until m. 40 shifts the center of gravity precariously close to the end of this passage, thereby creating an energetic impulsiveness that seems to urge the music forward just before the thematic group abates. In addition, the trumpets now prefigure not only the fateful climax of the movement, where the main theme is stripped down to its bare rhythm and hammered out with great force (mm. 369–89), but also the important device of paring motives down to their rhythmic skeleton.

Structural revisions

Bruckner's revision of the structure of the symphony can hardly be ascribed to any external motivation, Haas notwithstanding. Bruckner did shorten each movement by roughly 10 percent, but the symphony remained unusually lengthy. He also recomposed portions of each movement, most extensively in the first movement, the Trio, and the Adagio. (Table 5.1 outlines these changes.) These changes exhibit a compelling

Table 5.1 *Formal overview of the 1887 and 1890 versions*[a]

	1887 version	1890 version	Comments
	FIRST MOVEMENT		
Exposition			
A	1–50 (50)	1–50 (50)	
B	51–96 (46)	51–96 (46)	
C	97–128 (32)	97–128 (32)	
codetta	129–56 (28)	129–52 (24)	mm. 132 and 137–9 are removed.
Development			
part 1	157–72 (16)	153–68 (16)	
part 2	173–96 (24)	169–92 (24)	
part 3	197–232 (36)	193–224 (32)	mm. 205–24 are rewritten, shortened by four measures and their tonal scheme changed.
Recapitulation			
A	233–68 (36)	225–48 (24)	mm. 258–269 are removed.
Transition	269–92 (24)	249–82 (34)	This section is enlarged, revised, and its tonal plan is fundamentally altered.
A′	293–308 (16)	283–98 (16)	This passage is recomposed.
B	309–50 (42)	299–340 (42)	
C	351–402 (52)	341–92 (52)	The end of this section is reworked.
Coda			
part 1	403–23 (21)	393–417 (25)	Four concluding measures are added after m. 423.
part 2	424–53 (30)	nil	This loud, tutti conclusion is entirely removed.
total length	453	417	
	SECOND MOVEMENT		
	Scherzo		
A	1–66 (66)	1–64 (64)	mm. 25–6 are removed.
Development	67–144 (78)	65–134 (70)	mm. 89–90, 97–100, and 127–8 are removed.
A[1]	145–85 (42)	135–74 (40)	mm. 169–70 are removed.

Table 5.1 (*cont.*)

	1887 version	1890 version	Comments
Coda	186–211 (25)	175–95 (21)	mm. 207–10 are removed.
total	211	195	

		Trio	
a¹	1–16 (16)	1–16 (16)	Recomposed
a²	17–24 (8)	17–24 (8)	
b	25–48 (24)	25–44 (20)	mm. 41–4 are removed.
c	49–64 (16)	45–60 (16)	
a¹′	65–76 (12)	61–72 (12)	Recomposed
a²′	77–84 (8)	73–6 (4)	mm. 81–4 are removed.
b¹′	85–105 (21)	77–93 (17)	mm. 97–100 are removed.
total	105	93	

		THIRD MOVEMENT	
A Thematic group	1–46 (46)	1–46 (46)	
B Thematic group	47–81 (34)	47–81 (34)	
Transition 1	81–94 (14)	81–94 (14)	
A¹	95–150 (56)	95–140 (46)	mm. 132, 134, 138–9 and 143–50 are removed. Two bars are added after m. 142.
B¹	151–84 (34)	141–68 (28)	mm. 175–80 and mm. 181–4 are transposed up a step.
Transition 2	185–200 (16)	169–84 (16)	mm. 193–4 are removed, two bars are added after m. 200, and the tonal scheme of mm. 185–200 is revised.
A²	201–92 (92)	185–254 (70)	mm. 225–34, 282–8, and 292 are removed, and mm. 247–73 are rewritten, shortened, and their tonal scheme is altered.
B²	293–6 (4)	255–8 (4)	
Coda	297–329 (33)	259–91 (33)	
total	329	291	

Table 5.1 (*cont.*)

	1887 version	1890 version	Comments
	FOURTH MOVEMENT		
Exposition			
A	1–68 (68)	1–68 (68)	
B	69–146 (78)	69–134 (66)	mm. 119–30 are replaced by four new measures, and mm. 143–6 are removed.
C	147–222 (76)	135–210 (76)	
Codetta	223–84 (62)	211–52 (42)	mm. 223–42 are replaced by four new measures, and mm. 265–8 are removed.
Development			
part 1	285–312 (28)	253–84 (32)	mm. 305–12 are rewritten and expanded by four measures.
part 2	313–28 (16)	285–300 (16)	
part 3	329–72 (44)	301–44 (44)	
part 4	373–414 (42)	345–86 (42)	
part 5	415–64 (50)	387–436 (50)	
Recapitulation			
A	465–508 (44)	437–80 (44)	
Transition	509–82 (74)	481–546 (66)	mm. 517, 519, 521, 523, 553–4 and 558–9 are removed.
B	583–632 (50)	547–82 (36)	mm. 603–14 and 627–30 are removed, and mm. 625–6 are expanded to four measures.
C	633–702 (70)	583–646 (64)	mm. 687–90 and 701–2 are removed.
Coda	703–71 (69)	647–709 (63)	mm. 745–8 and 752–3 are removed.
total	771	709	

[a] This table draws in part on similar tables in Constantin Floros, "Die Fassungen der Achten Symphonie" in *Bruckner-Symposion: Die Fassungen*, ed. Franz Grasberger (Linz, 1981), 56, 59, and 61.

musical logic and it is wholly understandable that Bruckner felt that they improved the work.

The first movement

The structure of the exposition of this movement was largely untouched, but the rest of the movement was materially changed. The most dramatic alteration is the removal of the grand, triple-forte statement of the opening theme that ends the coda in the 1887 version. The original ending dramatically resolves the dissonant D♭ of the opening theme onto a blazing C major triad. The revised coda, in contrast, ends not with conclusive resolution, but poised quietly on C minor. Bruckner substantially revised the area surrounding the reprise as well. He shortened the approach to the reprise by four bars and altered its harmonic scheme slightly so that its initial phase emphasizes the dominant of C, not that of D♭ (see Example 5.1). This has the effect of solidifying the tonal framework of the entire mid-section of the movement by girding it at both ends with the dominant. Bruckner also slightly shortened the passage that ends the recapitulation of the main theme (mm. 258–69 of the 1887 version are removed) and altered its musical character. The original version of this passage (mm. 269–308 of the 1887 version) is complex in texture, with prominent rhythmic motives spiking the accompaniment. The revised version thins the texture, especially near the beginning (mm. 249–62 of the 1890 version), where the music is ominously spare, and in the medial climax (mm. 263–78), which crests with blunt simplicity through a pair of diminished seventh chords. Bruckner also tightened the tonal framework of the beginning of this passage by more strongly articulating the tonic–dominant frame in mm. 249–78 (note how the trumpets reiterate C [mm. 255–61] and then G [mm. 271–7] in the 1890 version). At the same time he made the following section, the reprise of the opening theme (mm. 279–98 in the 1890 version) against a tangled, dissonant A♭ background, more complexly ambiguous.

The second movement

The changes to the Scherzo are comparatively minor, comprising a few short excisions, some harmonic tinkering, and orchestral retouching. The revised Trio, in contrast, is fundamentally different. The tempo is

Example 5.1 First movement, approach to recapitulation,
1887 and 1890 versions compared
(a) 1887 version

(b) 1890 version

changed from Allegro Moderato to Langsam, thus creating a much
longer, slower interlude. Bruckner entirely recomposed the opening
theme (mm. 1–24). He preserved the B and C themes more or less intact,
but revised them so as to emphasize one of the most striking features of
the Trio, the passages of pure, major triadic stillness (first E, later A♭)
that dominate the latter portion of both halves of the movement. Bruckner clarified the harmonic preparation of these sections: the revised
opening of the trio contains flashes of C♭, the enharmonic dominant of
E, and the revised voice-leading points very directly to E. He also added
the distinctive harp flourishes that italicize E major (mm. 37–44), a
tonality that is rather striking within a C minor context and one that

comes to figure importantly in the symphony. Although E major is not heard in the first movement, after it appears in the Trio it plays a note-worthy role in the rest of the symphony: it is the key in which the B theme of the Adagio appears, it is the starting point of the two climactic "waves" later in that movement, and it begins the striking, "Feierlich, innig" passage that intrudes on the third thematic group of the Finale (1890 version, mm. 159–66). In addition, the revised Trio contains some important motivic links to the surrounding movements, most notably a trumpet call based on perfect intervals and a sixteenth–note triplet that recurs prominently in the Adagio (1890 version; Trio, mm. 26–39 and 85–7 and Adagio, mm. 237–8).[11]

The third movement

Bruckner's revisions to the Adagio are important. As in the opening movement, the first part of the movement is essentially unchanged. Much of the remainder (mm. 95–200 of the 1887 version and mm. 95–184 of the 1890 version) is, however, crucially modified. It is short-ened by the removal of several brief passages (see Table 5.1). The har-monic scheme of the second transition is modified (and this places renewed emphasis on the key of C; see the 1890 version, mm. 169–76). The sublime culminatory passage preceding the coda (1887 version, mm. 269–73; 1890 version, 239–43) is the single most elaborately reworked area of the entire symphony. Bruckner made several changes that intensify its power: he removed a gentle interlude of ten bars that dissipates some of the gathering energy of the early stages of the *Steige-rung* (1887 version, 225–34 [this is reinserted in Haas's version]); he deleted a forceful arrival on a D♭ 6/4 chord that anticipates the ultimate tonal goal and thus somewhat attenuates the accumulating tonal tension (mm. 253–4 of the 1887 version); he made the long preparatory har-monic ascent more inexorably goal-directed; he enriched the orchestral fabric of two tensely anticipatory passages (e.g., 1890 version, mm. 223–6 and 235–8) to such striking effect that, as Ernst Kurth wrote, the final version "appears 'more expressive' than the later 'Expression-ists.'"[12] Most importantly, Bruckner reoriented the terrible harmonic jolt that sunders the great final span of the movement. In the 1887 version the progression moves from the dominant of C to a triad on A♭;

Example 5.2 Adagio, climactic progression, 1887 and 1890 versions compared
(a) 1887 version

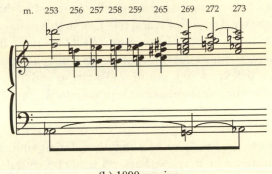

(b) 1890 version

in the 1890 version it is relocated up a minor third so that it moves from the dominant of E♭ to a triad on C♭ (see Example 5.2). It might sound, in the abstract, more *outré* for a movement in D♭ major to reach its high point, as the 1887 version does, on a cadential progression in C major than on one in E♭ major, as in the 1890 version. Yet in actuality, the revised version of this passage is more potent. In the first version the G that supports the C major cadential preparation in mm. 269–72 functions as a lower neighbor to the A♭ (which is, of course, the dominant of D♭) that controls both ends of the passage; thus, the move to the dominant of C major feels like a move away from the movement's prevailing tonal region, and the powerfully articulated irregular progression from the dominant of C to A♭ (mm. 272–3) has the effect of returning the music to its "proper" orbit around the ultimate tonic, D♭. In the 1890 version, this whole passage is harmonically renovated so that it begins and ends in the tonal region of E and B (=C♭). In this tonal context, the arrival on B♭ (as dominant of E♭) in mm. 239–42 is a move from a relatively distant region into a domain closer to the tonic, and thus the subsequent sudden deflection to C♭ in m. 243 pulls us suddenly away, and leaves us perched on a strange harmonic promontory.

The fourth movement

The revisions to the Finale are of a slightly different kind. The movement was shortened by sixty-two bars, primarily by several short excisions, but Bruckner left the fundamental structure and design of the movement intact. With only a few minor exceptions (i.e., the substitution of new four-bar passages for mm. 119–30 and 223–42 of the 1887 version and the rewriting of mm. 305–12) Bruckner's revisions involve no recomposition; indeed the composer was able simply to enter most of his changes directly into his original score of the 1887 version.[13] Even the orchestration, which already included triple woodwind, was only lightly revised. The relatively minor nature of the changes made in this movement shows Bruckner's independence of mind. The Finale was the object of Levi's sharpest criticism (he called it a "closed book"), yet Bruckner's revisions can hardly be considered a response to this criticism. Nowhere did he alter the basic design of the movement; he did nothing to open it to Levi's understanding. Rather, he stuck closely to his original conception of the movement that he had called "the most important of my life."

The motivation and meaning of Bruckner's revisions

Bruckner's revisions have been interpreted variously. The common opinion, that Bruckner had intended largely to make the work more easily playable or practically acceptable, has been widely overvalued. The 1890 version is, as we have seen, hardly simplified and it failed to help the symphony win performances. Not only did Levi eschew performing the symphony despite Bruckner's urgings, but Weingartner's decision to abandon the work in 1891 hinged on its difficulty. As he wrote to Levi: "unfortunately I couldn't perform the Bruckner. The symphony offers such difficulties that I could not demand the necessary rehearsals."[14] Bruckner himself realized that the revised Eighth surpassed the technical capacities of most orchestras; in 1893 he actually advised his old mentor Otto Kitzler not to attempt a performance with his provincial orchestra in Brno, which Bruckner thought inadequate to the task.[15]

One relatively minor aspect of Bruckner's revision has been inadequately recognized. The 1887 version was largely composed, if not fully orchestrated, before Bruckner reordered the movements and placed the Scherzo second and the Adagio third, and in some details this version retains the impress of the original sequence of movements. Some of the revisions contained in the 1890 version – most importantly the changed coda of the first movement and the new Trio – seem in part subtle responses to the new tonal scheme created by the new order of movements. The original fortissimo coda of the first movement is the clearest vestige of this early phase of the symphony's evolution. When the Adagio followed immediately, as it originally did, this emphatic tonic conclusion (with its strongly drawn resolution of D♭ as an auxiliary of C) served as an important point of contrast to the subsequent movement in D♭. With the relocation of the Scherzo, which ends with a vigorous cadence in C, the first movement was freed of this obligation and could safely end in quiet mystery. Similarly, the 1890 Trio seems designed with the new sequence of movements in mind. With its unusual slow tempo and expressive intensity the revised Trio is, in effect, a harbinger of the slow movement, and this premonitory quality is deepened by Bruckner's late addition of harps, which were already installed in the Adagio, and by the newly added motivic anticipation of the Adagio's climax. In contrast, the initial version of the Adagio, with a culmination that momentarily holds out the promise of a cadence in C (mm. 269–72), seems more naturally to precede the Scherzo with its frank C minor beginning than the tonally ambivalent opening pages of the Finale.

The 1890 version also raises questions about the broader significance of Bruckner's revisions. These questions have been thoughtfully engaged by a few scholars, notably Manfred Wagner and Bryan Gilliam. Both Wagner and Gilliam recognize, albeit from different angles, that Bruckner's revisions embody the composer's renewed concern to reach his potential audiences. Wagner proposed, with a categorical sweep of the hand, that the first versions of Bruckner's symphonies were composed with "no consideration" for orchestral practicalities or "acoustic economy," and were not conceived in terms of audience response.[16] He pointed to a number of passages in the first versions of the Eighth and, especially, the Third and Fourth Symphonies that seem too busily cluttered and dense with musical information ("informationsreich") to convey their sense in a concert hall. This proposal is, undoubtedly, more apt in regard to the Third and Fourth Symphonies, the earliest versions of which date from a time when Bruckner's radical symphonic style was not yet fully mature; Bruckner did, of course, revise both of these symphonies over the course of some fifteen years, each time making the score more obviously effective. The Eighth is a rather different case (not only is it a fully mature work, but its revision followed the initial composition relatively soon), yet Wagner's sense that Bruckner's revisions clarify and focus the musical design and symphonic texture does explain at least some aspects of the reworking. The 1890 version does tone down the few places in the 1887 version where the orchestration is gloriously "uneconomical" (e.g., the coda of the first movement), the texture fussier than necessary (e.g., Adagio, mm. 185–94 and 293–4) or the musical progression slightly awkward (e.g., first movement mm. 263–307). Gilliam reads Bruckner's revisions as an attempt to make the symphony more acceptable to the conservative musical tastes of the time; he suggested provocatively that the revised version of the Eighth was designed to heighten the work's potential appeal to the Hanslick/Brahms audience by making it "more logical" and, in places, more "streamlined." Ultimately this effort was, in Gilliam's view, misguided. By ameliorating some of the work's grandiosity and "sheer massiveness" – which as Gilliam rightly pointed out are "words foreign to the Hanslickian vocabulary" and are "still often viewed with suspicion in modern critical discourse" – Bruckner wrongly measured "his work by a standard other than his own," and thus in some measure "compromised boldness for coherence."[17]

I share Wagner's and Gilliam's sense that the 1890 version reflects a heightened concern with effect of the piece on the audience; clearly, with its greater concentration and sharper lines, the revision presents a more imposing face than does the 1887 version. Rather than compromising the symphony's boldness, then, the revisions sharpen it by drawing the music at times more daringly and at times more carefully. The 1890 version is, in other words, less striking for any taint of accommodation than for its intensification and concentration of characteristics that were already present, if less vividly, in the 1887 version. To take one significant example: one of the symphony's characteristic gestures is a long climactic ascent that at its height deflects in some way, and in some cases even rives the musical fabric; the two great examples are the reprise of the main theme in the first movement (1890 version, m. 225) and the tremendous climax preceding the coda in the Adagio (1890 version, mm. 239–43). In his revision, as we have seen, Bruckner intensified both of these passages. In the first movement, he accomplished this primarily by changing the preparation of the recapitulation: he focused the harmony more closely on the dominant of the tonic, C minor, and this heightened the tonal impact of the arrival of the primary theme. In the Adagio, Bruckner similarly modified the apex of the movement to make its harmonic effect more overwhelming and tightened its preparatory build-up by removing some passages that momentarily lower the tension, thus creating a longer, more unbroken, and therefore more unyielding, period of intensification – this, in turn, creates a greater effect when the anticipated culmination is subverted at the last moment. Bruckner made a few simpler revisions that tighten passages of gathering force in the first movement and the Finale as well (in the first movement compare mm. 217–25 of the 1887 version with mm. 213–16 of the 1890 version, and in the Finale mm. 515–24 of the 1887 version with mm. 487–92 of the 1890 version). These revisions do in a sense "smooth out the nooks and crannies," as Gilliam writes, but in context they have the effect not of planing but of honing the formal dynamics of the piece.[18] Even the revision of the massive accompaniment to the insistent trumpet calls that sound near the end of the first movement, which as Gilliam points out is undoubtedly more static and less sweeping, exhibits a similar logic. The revised version, which reduces the chromatically inflected three-octave upward sweep of the original (1887 version, mm. 379–95) in favor of a diatonic complex based on reiterated tetrachordal units (1890 version, mm. 369–85), may be less extravagant, yet it is more compactly coiled and its pure diatonicism not only adds to the air of austere tragedy, but also makes the triple-forte arrival and subsequent resolution of an augmented-sixth chord an event of rare decision (mm. 381–5).

Example 5.3 Adagio, passage leading to coda,
1887 and 1890 versions compared
(a) 1887 version

(b) 1890 version

As well as reshaping climactic sections, Bruckner's revisions heighten a very different aspect of the symphony. In addition to loudly grand passages, the Eighth Symphony is characterized by stretches of remarkably still, quiet music, the greatest of which is the marvelous coda to the Adagio, thirty-three bars that unfurl with glorious self-possession above a long tonic pedal. Episodes of relative stillness occur, if less dramatically, elsewhere too (e.g., 1890 version, first movement, mm. 140–64; Scherzo, mm. 115–34; Finale, mm. 45–69), and in the 1890 version, Bruckner subtly highlighted some of them. His removal of the loud ending of the first movement, for example, grants new importance to the quiet passage that now ends it and thus foreshadows the peaceful coda of the Adagio rather than the triumphant close of the Finale. In the revised Trio, the new broad tempo obviously creates an additional reservoir of slow, still music, and magnifies its several ruminative triadic areas (mm. 37–44 and 85–93).

The genius of Bruckner's revision is fully present even in small things. In the 1890 version the four bars preceding the coda of the Adagio are modified with lapidary skill, so that the musical character of this passage is not changed but rather revealed to us with greater acuity (see Example 5.3). The harmonically full accompaniment of the 1887 version is reduced, and simply eliminated in the first bar; the initial dynamic marking is lowered to *piano*; and the woodwind countermelody is trimmed. As the vehicle of the movement's final authentic cadence and as the only statement of the contrasting theme in the tonic key – a traditional gesture of formal consummation – this juncture is naturally meaningful. The revised version, with its reticence to grant an explicit tonic triad, subtly underplays this significance and slyly makes resolution wait until the coda. Moreover, by leaving a slender melodic fragment to stand alone for a long moment poised on the brink of the tonic, the revision renders its poignancy far more keenly.

The 1892 edition, authorship, and performance practice

The first published edition of the Eighth Symphony has long been out of print, and its contents and history are veiled in some mystery. This much is clear: the symphony was first published in March 1892 by the firm of Haslinger–Schlesinger–Lienau (Berlin and Vienna) and although the published text is based on the 1890 version, it differs in some ways from the text preserved in Bruckner's final manuscript (which is reproduced by Nowak's critical edition of the 1890 version). These differences include a cut of six bars in the Finale (following m. 92), the repetition of two bars later in that movement (mm. 519–20 of Nowak's edition are repeated), some changes in the orchestration, and the addition of many tempo, dynamic, expression, and agogic markings (see Appendix B). The 1892 edition also contains two suggested cuts, marked "vi–de" above the staves, which if taken would result in the excision of mm. 262–78 of the first movement and mm. 519–76 (which correspond to mm. 523–580 of the 1890 version) of the Finale.

Authorship

The 1892 edition is now almost universally rejected as "inauthentic" and its textual differences, like those found in all of the first printed editions of Bruckner's works, are generally assumed to be the result of illegitimate editorial changes made without Bruckner's consent and possibly even without his awareness. While this is the case with several editions published in the last three years of Bruckner's life (notably the Masses in E minor and F minor and the Fifth Symphony, not to mention Ferdinand Löwe's posthumous edition of the Ninth Symphony published in 1903), a blanket dismissal of the editions published during his lifetime is too broad and categorical. Recent research has shown that the published versions of the Fourth Symphony (1888) and the Second Symphony (1892), which traditionally have been summarily dismissed, are, by any reasonable standard, authentic.[1] As the real complexity and ambiguity surrounding the texts, both manuscript and printed, of Bruckner's works becomes evident, it also grows increasingly apparent that our view of the first printed editions of Bruckner's music has long been controlled by an elaborate mythology about their inauthenticity. It has become a virtual article of faith that Bruckner's music was altered illegitimately by various editors and that the editions of his music published during his lifetime are as a result simply not authentic.[2]

In a different context, Garry Wills recently wrote, with unintended applicability to the Bruckner case, that "a myth does not take hold without expressing many truths – misleading truths, usually, but important ones," including "truth to the demand for some control over complex realities."[3] The myths we have constructed about Bruckner editions, their authorship, and their nature and significance are not without some basis (witness the duplicity involved in the editing of the F minor Mass and the Fifth Symphony), but they have given us a control over complex realities that is often too easy and thus both illusory and artificial. In this light, we need to rethink our estimation of the 1892 edition of the Eighth Symphony. Any positive determination of its precise authorship is not now possible. In part this is because substantial documentary research remains to be done: to this day no thorough study and collation of the extensive manuscript sources of the Eighth Symphony – which number more than forty items in Vienna, Munich, Kremsmünster, and Washington – has been undertaken (neither Haas nor Nowak published a critical report); in particular, the manuscript copy used in the preparation of the printed score needs to be examined.[4] Yet even an exhaustive study of all the pertinent sources cannot answer the decisive questions about the text of the 1892 edition. It is not, of course, possible to prove definitively that Bruckner was *not* responsible for the revisions it contains; even those not in his hand might have been made at his express instruction. More importantly, pure documentary research cannot by itself produce critical and interpretive judgments; in order to come to a reasonable appraisal of this text, it is necessary to uncover the circumstances through which it originated and to evaluate the nature and significance of its musical substance.

The origins of the 1892 edition

In 1891, when the Eighth Symphony was to be published, Josef Schalk and Max von Oberleithner were charged with the task of seeing the score through press. Apparently, Schalk took on the musical preparation of the *Stichvorlage* (the score used by the printer), while Oberleithner handled arrangements with the publisher and corrected the proofs.[5] The manuscript used was a copy prepared by Christ and Hofmeyer, likely the one prepared in 1890, shortly after Bruckner finished the composition of the revised version.[6] (This was also probably the score sent to Weingartner for use in his aborted performance in 1891.)

The crucial questions concern the revisions that were made to the text before it was sent to the publisher. Schalk's correspondence makes it immediately evident that he and Oberleithner edited the score. In a letter of 31 July 1891 he informed Oberleithner that "after a week of extremely strenuous work I have finally made the score of the Finale ready for printing [*druckreif*]."[7] Five days later, Schalk wrote again to Oberleithner; this letter contains a pair of frequently cited statements. Schalk wrote that in the Finale the "six bars before F [i.e., the six bars following m. 92] *must also be omitted in print*. The entirely unmotivated reminiscence of [Symphony no.] Seven primarily led me to decide to remove it."[8] These bars are, in fact, deleted in the 1892 edition, and they do resemble mm. 197–202 of the first movement of the Seventh Symphony, but it is unclear why Schalk would have considered this grounds for removal. Schalk must also have been influenced by the fact that Bruckner himself had removed the corresponding spot in the recapitulation in the 1890 version (compare mm. 547–66 of the 1890 version). Whatever its rationale, it is likely that the decision to cut these measures from the 1892 edition was Schalk's. Not only did Schalk say so, but the revision is so crude as to suggest that it was not made by Bruckner. The six bars are simply stricken with no attempt to splice the music together smoothly. A more careful editor (i.e., Bruckner himself) might well have changed the final note in the bass in m. 92 from E♭ to D and might have removed the crescendo in the second half of this bar since it now leads nowhere, or he might have simply started the cut four bars earlier as Bruckner had done at the corresponding spot in the recapitulation in the 1890 version (compare at m. 567 of that version).

In the same letter Schalk also requested that Oberleithner "pursue [*treiben*] the corrections only with the publisher. If Bruckner has to read from the cut [*gestrichenen*] score at a rehearsal all of our good intentions will be thwarted, and instead of his thanks we would probably earn his curse." Several scholars have taken these sentences as evidence of extreme, surreptitious editorial intervention by Schalk and Oberleithner, and have even used this letter as support for the conclusion that the revisions contained in the 1892 edition are simply illegitimate.[9] It is likely, however, that we are faced here with an instance in which the reigning mythology about Bruckner editions has fostered misinterpretation. First, the word "gestrichenen [cut]" has traditionally been transcribed inaccurately as "geschriebenen [written]," thus rendering the meaning of the sentence not only rather obscure but also apparently more damning by creating the implication that the entire "written score," meaning presumably the *Stichvorlage*, contained changes that Schalk wanted to hide from Bruckner.[10] Furthermore, Schalk's letters to Oberleithner contain additional passages, which have been glossed over, that both explain the cryptic reference to the "gestrichenen" score and contravene any simple dismissal of their editorial activities as unauthorized meddling.[11] These passages reveal that Schalk and Oberleithner did not work in secrecy, but discussed at least some things with Bruckner, and, moreover, they show that Bruckner did not automatically accept suggested changes. In the 31 July letter, Schalk proposed a "very suitable" and "easily effected" cut before rehearsal letter Pp in the Finale. No music is actually removed at this place in the 1892 edition, but it does contain a suggestion (marked "vi–de") to cut *ad libitum* from six bars after Kk to Pp (this means in effect jumping from m. 522 to m. 581 of the Nowak edition). Schalk apparently would have been happy to remove this passage: he argued the merits of this excision to Oberleithner ("all that is lost is a rather superfluous build-up and the repetition of the anyhow very prolonged chorale-like lyrical thematic group [*Gesangsperiode*]") and in his four-hand piano reduction Schalk did simply leave out this passage.[12] So apparently Schalk had some scruples about actually excising this long stretch of music in the orchestral score, or perhaps he anticipated that Bruckner would not accept it. In any case, he instructed Oberleithner that "in print the whole must, I suppose, be included," which of course is what happened. Schalk's second letter states, somewhat cryptically, that "we must undo [the cut] at Letter Z! . . . I have already discussed the retention [of this passage] with the Master and he agreed entirely." Taken by itself this reference is unclear, but it can be explained with reference to a loose sheet of paper inserted in Bruckner's manuscript score of the 1890 version (A-Wn Mus. Hs. 19.480) that, as Dermot Gault reports, "carries a proposal to cut. . . from the 'Ruhig' episode [i.e., at Z] to just before letter Aa [i.e., mm. 345–86]. . . and substitute four bars of timpani roll."[13] This was probably one of the cuts that Bruckner had suggested to Weingartner in early 1891, and presumably Oberleithner (or less likely Schalk) had actually crossed out this passage in the *Stichvorlage* before Bruckner made it clear that he did not want this stretch eliminated from the printed score. (Bruckner had of course already made this clear to Weingartner in his letter of 27 March 1891; see Chapter 2.) This also explains Schalk's anxiety that Bruckner not see the "gestrichenen" score; he was worried that it would reveal that he and Oberleithner had made the big cut after Z (which was soon undone), and also possibly the shorter one after m. 92, before clearing it with Bruckner.

If some of the revisions, notably cuts, in the 1892 edition were made (or not made) contingent on Bruckner's prior approval, others were apparently not. In the letter of 31 July 1891 Schalk made it clear that he had made numerous changes on his own initiative and, with a scrupulousness that belies the image of him as a shameless bowdlerizer, he acknowledged that these pushed the limits of propriety: "The many alterations [I have made], which appear to me to be completely necessary, can be justified only through the most painstaking conscientiousness. You will easily recognize the intention toward greater clarity of effect or expression that [the revisions] contain . . . May the same conviction, which I have now gained, console you with the thought that the matter is extremely important and actually saves the life of this work. I assure you that I've done only what is absolutely necessary; I had to leave much unchanged in view of the irresponsibility of the project."

We are faced then with something of a puzzle: the 1892 score almost certainly contains changes – the cut after m. 92 of the Finale and possibly the new layer of performance indications and the few instrumental retouchings – that were made by Schalk without Bruckner's direct involvement. Although Schalk felt that these changes verged on the "irresponsible," it is far from certain that he kept them secret from

Bruckner (remember, he expressed worry only that Bruckner might see the "gestrichenen" manuscript, not the revised text itself). Although Bruckner may, as Hawkshaw wrote, have been *"deliberately removed* [emphasis original]" from the preparation of the editions of the F minor mass and the Fifth Symphony, we are not justified in making that claim about the 1892 edition of the Eighth Symphony.[14] Rather, this case seems more closely analogous with those of the two other symphonies published between 1889 and 1892, namely the Fourth and the Third, in which Bruckner approvingly left part of the process – exactly how much can probably never be determined – of preparing the text for publication, including adding a final layer of performance markings, to an amanuensis.[15] Although the documentary history of the 1892 edition of the Eighth Symphony has not yet been worked out in detail, its origins appear to be similar and clearly involved a degree of collaboration in the final stages of editing. But this collaboration was presumably done only with Bruckner's consent. Indeed, Franz Schalk later said that Bruckner himself edited the revised text of the Eighth and Josef von Wöss stated that Bruckner had authorized the published edition.[16]

The textual situation of the Eighth Symphony is messy and cannot support simple, black-and-white answers; so, while the 1892 edition may not be "pure Bruckner" – whatever that might be – to all appearances Bruckner authorized it, and for that reason it needs to be taken seriously. If we simply dismiss the 1892 edition in the name of honoring Bruckner's "real intention," we paradoxically do something that contradicts the composer's own actions. For much of this century claims about Bruckner's true, inner wishes have often been used in this way to defend the exclusive preserve of modern Urtext editions, to stifle debate about the "Bruckner Problem," and to trump, legitimately or not, more complex answers. This process has obscured what is, as we shall see, an extremely valuable and historically important tradition of Bruckner performance and interpretation.

Notation, performance practice, and interpretation

In trying to come to understand the 1892 edition it is essential to bear in mind that it – far more than Bruckner's manuscripts – is a score designed for practical use; thus, if nothing else, this text does undoubtedly present a fascinating and valuable picture of nineteenth-century interpretations of the work. It explains how the music should sound and go far more explicitly – and in a musically compelling way – than do Bruckner's manuscript scores of the 1890 and 1887 versions and the modern critical editions based on them. This new, more careful and extensive notation of performance indications is consistent with Bruckner's practice with the other editions published in the late 1880s and early 1890s. It was also only during the late 1880s, with the growing success of the Seventh Symphony and later the Fourth and Third, that Bruckner began to gain extensive knowledge of how his symphonies actually worked in repeated public performances. As Manfred Wagner pointed out, Bruckner had little first-hand experience with the orchestra until relatively late in his adulthood, and his early manuscript scores do not reflect a practiced orchestral hand in their notation of performance instructions and details of instrumentation.[17] Several of Bruckner's statements make it clear that he was aware of these shortcomings. Before the first performance of the Seventh Symphony (which was based on Bruckner's manuscript score), he wrote to the conductor, Arthur Nikisch, "in the score many important, frequent tempo changes are not marked."[18] (When the score of the Seventh Symphony was published in 1885, it contained some added tempo markings, clearly designed to remedy the lack Bruckner pointed out to Nikisch.) Similarly, during rehearsal of the Eighth Symphony, Bruckner felt compelled to ask Weingartner to "please freely modify the tempi (as necessary for clarity)."[19] It was undoubtedly in order to avoid leaving important decisions about tempi to the discretion of conductors, which obviously admitted substantial room for misinterpretation, that Bruckner made sure to delineate clearly – far more so than in his unpublished manuscripts – the overall tempo schemes in the published editions of his works.

Unlike the Third and Fourth Symphonies (and, for that matter, the Seventh, First, and Second), the Eighth was not performed before it was published. Ordinarily performances afforded Bruckner a chance to make minor adjustments (this was indeed the case with the Second and Fourth Symphonies for example).[20] Although the composer was not to hear a note of the Eighth for nearly two years, Weingartner's aborted performance in early 1891 did provide him with at least some practical second-hand information. This experience must have shown Bruckner that his manuscript text of the 1890 version did not adequately represent his conception of the symphony in one crucial respect: it failed to explain fully how to handle some important matters of performance, above all, the dynamic balance of the various choirs of the orchestra, the overall tempo schemes, and local changes of tempo. These are exactly the areas addressed by the revisions contained in the 1892 edition, all of which – the added tempo and dynamic markings, the minor changes to the orchestration, and even the suggested cuts – relate to performance. In light of the great difficulty that both Levi and Weingartner had in coming to grips with the score, which they knew only in manuscript, it is easy to understand why Bruckner felt the need to provide future interpreters with more adequate instructions about tempi and dynamics, as well as some minor instrumental changes.

Instrumentation

As Appendix B shows, the revisions made to the orchestration in the 1892 editions are generally subtle; they are not nearly as extensive as the revisions Bruckner made in reworking the 1887 version. (The tendency among reviewers and commentators of referring casually to the "wholesale reorchestrations" found in the first editions of Bruckner's symphonies is a mere reflex, and is not borne out by the facts.) Aside from the reorchestration of mm. 637–43 of the Finale, only the additions to the timpani part in mm. 445–6, 453–4, and 461–2 of the Finale and the added cymbal crash in m. 479 of the same movement are striking. In some sections, different string techniques   pizzicato, mutes, tremolando – are incorporated. Occasional doublings are added, more often for reasons of clarity than of color; see, for example, the doubling of the cellos and basses with bassoons in mm. 132–9 of the first movement, or the addition of horns in mm. 331–2 of the Finale to support a poorly articulated bass–line. Another change made to clarify an important passage is the deployment of the woodwinds on the final pages of the Finale (mm. 688–96) to double the climactic trumpet fanfares. None of these changes to the orchestration alters the basic character of the music, and they certainly do not represent a conceptual change. They simply strengthen and clarify what was already present.

Dynamics

In his manuscript Bruckner followed an older method of notating dynamics: even in passages scored for a large and diverse group of instruments, he indicated only one dynamic level for all of the parts. This notation was standard for much of the nineteenth century (cf. the orchestral scores of Beethoven, Schubert, Schumann, and Brahms), and it assumes, as Erich Leinsdorf explained, that adjustments of the relative loudness of the different instruments would be made by the conductor: "balances are so obvious most of the time that no composer writing in the classical manner dreamed of taking time for such minute and self-evident [notational] detail" as indicating graded dynamics for the various instrumental groups.[21] Bruckner's use of the orchestra departs quite decisively from the classical manner, and balancing his scoring, especially with its great use of brass instruments, is not easily done. When Weingartner was rehearsing the Eighth, he wrote to Bruckner complaining of the sonic predominance of the brass and winds (which he diplomatically ascribed to his small body of strings) and even asked if he could remove some of the doublings in the winds and brass.[22] Bruckner agreed provided Weingartner did not alter the score or parts.[23] The 1892 edition remedies this problem. It does not lighten the scoring in even the most powerful tutti passages, but it does consistently modify the dynamics. Brass are frequently notated one level lower than the strings and woodwinds (e.g., *forte* brass with *fortissimo* strings and woodwinds).[24] In this way, the published score merely spells out what any conscientious conductor must do. Franz Schalk, who was an internationally esteemed conductor in the first three decades of the twentieth century, wrote that the brass and strings need different dynamic levels "because otherwise in Bruckner's instrumentation the brass will obscure the strings."[25] This disparity was greatest in the days of gut strings, which do not project as brilliantly as do modern wound strings. Yet even in the modern era, the great Bruckner conductor Eugen Jochum (1902–87) reached the same conclusion as did Schalk: "even when the brass and strings play the same thing in a *fortissimo* the brass must be handled with restraint . . . The brass will come across anyway, the strings must be brought out."[26]

Table 6.1 *The tempo scheme of the exposition of the finale in the 1890 version and the 1892 edition*

	1890 version (ed. Nowak)	1892 edition
m. 1	Feierlich, nicht schnell (half-note = 69 MM)	Feierlich, nicht schnell (half-note = 69 MM)
m. 69	Langsamer (half-note = 60 MM)	Langsamer (half-note = 60 MM)
m. 99	Noch langsamer	Noch etwas langsamer
m. 111	a tempo	a tempo
m. 135		Erstes Zeitmaß
m. 150		poco ritard.
m. 151		a tempo
m. 159	Feierlich, innig	Feierlich, innig
m. 183		Erstes Zeitmaß
m. 206		poco accel.
m. 208		rit.
m. 209		a tempo
m. 221		etwas zurückhaltend
m. 223		a tempo
m. 229		zurückhaltend
m. 231		a tempo (ruhig)

Tempo markings

Tempi are of particular importance in articulating the expansive and often episodic forms of the Eighth Symphony, yet apt tempi are not always immediately evident from the music, and Bruckner's manuscript scores (and thus Haas's and Nowak's editions), with their sparing and inconsistent tempo indications, provide only partial answers. Bruckner noted most of the main tempi and, confusingly, some but not all of the major tempo changes. In Bruckner's original manuscript the opening theme group of the Finale is marked "Feierlich, nicht schnell" (half-note = 69 MM); a slower tempo ("Langsamer," half-note = 60 MM) is clearly marked for the second theme (m. 69), as is another slowdown ("Noch langsamer") at m. 99 and the subsequent resumption of the "langsamer" tempo (m. 111); yet Bruckner gives no further instruction with the beginning of the third theme in m. 135 (see Table 6.1).[27] Taken absolutely literally, this means that the "langsamer" tempo should continue until the next marked return of the main tempo one hundred and sixty-six bars later. Surely this is impossible; not only would the music drag terribly, but it would rob the "Feierlich, innig" passage at m. 159 of some of its special character. The 1892 edition is much more detailed and leaves little to guesswork; it is noteworthy how carefully it prescribes the resumption of the original tempo for the third theme (m. 135) and after each ritard. Constantin Floros was right to say that in Bruckner's autograph scores the "sparse tempo indications are not always sufficient for a meaningful performance" and, as Floros demonstrated, conductors generally do not even try to follow them slavishly.[28] Even so, modern-day Bruckner conductors do at times evince some difficulty in finding just tempi and even more in working out the apt and convincing tempo relationships – a problem that is effectively resolved in the 1892 edition.

In addition to large-scale tempo schemes, numerous local fluctuations of tempo are indicated in the 1892 score. For example, occasional momentary italicizations are spelled out, as in mm. 221 and 229 of the Finale where the tempo is broadened to highlight the flute chords. Several passages are punctuated by instructions to hold back momentarily and then resume the main tempo, thus shaping the flow of relatively large musical paragraphs (see, for example, the several "ritard. – a tempo" indications in the second thematic group of the first movement reprise [mm. 299–340]). This device is also used to introduce musical events that do not involve a basic tempo change (see for example, the onset of the second thematic group of the Adagio, mm. 47 and 141). Perhaps the most striking of the tempo indications in this score are its many prolonged accelerandi that accompany Bruckner's characteristic *Steigerungen*, passages that climb toward a culminating point of arrival by building in intensity, loudness, register, and harmonic and surface rhythm (good examples are the prolonged approaches to the climaxes in the Adagio discussed in Chapter 4 and the build-up to the reprise of the opening theme in the first movement [mm. 201–24]). In Bruckner's manuscript these passages are marked only with long crescendi, while in the printed score they are additionally marked with progressive increases of tempo. As Robert Philip has shown, this application of accelerandi is a typical "nineteenth-century" interpretation of this sort of passage: modern performers are strongly inclined to eschew prominent accelerandi.[29] Thus, as with the other performance instructions added to the 1892 edition, such written accelerandi undoubtedly *do not* represent a new conception of the pieces, but simply make explicit what Bruckner left implicit in his manuscript text.

The tempo notations in the 1892 edition describe a rhetorical give and take that is wholly typical of progressive, late nineteenth-century interpretive ideas. For example in *On Conducting* (1869) Wagner wrote in detail of the need for "well-considered modifications of the tempo," which are just as necessary "as the correct intonation of the notes themselves, if an intelligible rendering is to be obtained." Wagner wrote that the artful manipulation of the tempo was particularly important in pieces of moderate pace (e.g., "sehr mäßig bewegt") and in which "the themes are treated episodically," a category that contains many of Bruckner's symphonic movements.[30] Since almost all of Bruckner's early champions (Richter, Levi, Nikisch, Mottl, and the Schalk brothers), not to mention the composer himself, were Wagnerians, they would have shared the belief that the successful performance of music entailed rhetorical and structural adjustments of tempo, another hint that tempi modifications added in the 1892 editions probably do not add something that was previously entirely absent from the music. Franz Schalk's comments from the 1920s on the performance indications in the printed version of Bruckner's scores help place the whole issue in proper historical perspective. He explained that when Bruckner's symphonies began to appear in concert in the 1880s, Kapellmeisters still followed the "'rigid system [*starre System*]'" marked by "an inflexible tempo," "dynamics with little transitional shading" and little "concern for thematic clarity in performance."[31] The markings in Bruckner's published score were intended, it would seem, largely to ward off the stiff, severe style of interpretation that prevailed in the 1880s (and as we shall see, perhaps in the 1980s, too). If, in an age of virtuosic, visionary conductors, Schalk felt called upon to emphasize that these tempo indications should not "be given too much weight," today, in an age with a rather more abstemious interpretive ethos, we might well invert Schalk's concern, and stress that they should not simply be forgotten or ignored.

Changing interpretive approaches and their significance
(a short case study)

The musical implications of the performance markings in the 1892 edition become vividly apparent when they are studied in conjunction with an array of recordings made over the past sixty years. The reprise of the third thematic group in the Finale (mm. 579–642; compare mm. 583–646 of the 1890 version) can serve as a concise example for such a survey. This passage begins quietly with a series of fugal entries of the head motive of the third theme in the violas and violins above a sustained timpani roll on the dominant. As the strings continue to spin out this motivic material, the clarinets, oboes, horns, and flutes enter in turn as the music gradually builds to a powerful *fortissimo* arrival (m. 617) above a big dominant pedal, whereupon the trombones, trumpets, and bass tuba proclaim the opening theme of the first movement. From this peak the music recedes until it comes to rest with a series of three *pianissimo* timpani strokes on G. The manuscript text of the 1890 version of this passage contains relatively complete instructions regarding dynamics, while tempo indications are all but absent. In marked contrast, the 1892 edition presents a detailed set of instructions for the temporal progress of the passage that effectively describe the desired dramatic shape (see Table 6.2): the music is to begin calmly, very gradually increase in tempo and volume, peak vigorously, and then slow and grow ever calmer as it comes to rest. (Note too that the 1892 tempo markings spell out a continual process, not a series of states: beginning very calmly, very gradually growing more lively, etc.) The few changes to the orchestration found on these pages in the 1892 edition also contribute to the dynamism of the music. The percussiveness of the pizzicato cellos in mm. 609–16 helps to propel the music, and the more extensive use of tremolo in the cellos (mm. 601–6 and mm. 627–31) and violas (mm. 627–30) contributes to the surging and ebbing flow of the music by increasing the vibrating energy of the climax. (The reorchestration of mm. 637–44, where an oboe, two clarinets, two horns, and tremolando violin supplant the violins and viola of the 1890 version, is a simple change of timbre.)

Recordings reveal a clear historical trend. Older conductors, especially those who were active in the first decades of this century, tended to shape these pages in ways reminiscent of the 1892 edition (and to a degree that

Table 6.2 *Performance indications in mm. 583–646 of the Finale in the 1890 version and the 1892 edition*

	1890 version (ed. Nowak)	1892 edition
m. 583	viel langsamer (*p*)	sehr ruhig beginnend
m. 589	cresc.	cresc.
m. 592	dim. (*p*)	dim. (*p*)
m. 593		sehr allmählich belebend
m. 595	cresc.	cresc.
m. 601	poco a poco cresc. (*pp*)	poco a poco cresc. ed accelerando (*pp*)
m. 609	(*p*)	accel. (*p*)
m. 613	(*f*)	cresc. (*mf*)
m. 615	cresc.	cresc.
m. 617	(*ff*)	Lebhaft (*ff*)
m. 622	langsam	zurückhaltend
m. 623	Tempo I (*p*)	a tempo / dim.
m. 627	(*p*)	zurückhaltend und immer ruhiger werdend (*p*)
m. 635	dim. sempre	dim.
m. 637	(*f*)	(*p*)
m. 640		dim. (*p*)
m. 641	(*f*)	(*p*)

Dynamic markings are in parentheses; measure numbers follow the Nowak edition.

might well strike modern sensibilities as extreme); recordings by conductors of younger generations are generally much less rhetorical and far steadier in tempo (see Table 6.3). For example, recordings from the 1940s (which are the oldest that exist) typically present this passage as a grand accelerando–rallentando, with a tempo increase of as much as 20 percent. (Karajan's 1944 recording is a notable exception.) Equally important in these performances are the waxing and waning of sonic intensity of the orchestral playing, the incisiveness of the phrasing, and the increasing rhythmic animation that accompany these tempo modifications; the music drives forcefully toward the climax, crests, and then subsides. Recorded performances of the 1892 score by Bruno Walter (1876–1962) and Hans

Table 6.3 *A comparison of tempi in performances of mm. 583–646 of the Finale*

	mm. 583–90	mm. 609–16	mm. 637–40
Walter[a] NYP/1941	MM 56	72	60
Karajan[b] Berlin Staatskapelle/1944	MM 56	51	44
Furtwängler[b] VPO/1944	MM 53	65	40
Furtwängler[b] BPO/1949	MM 55	65	37
Jochum[b] Hamburg/1949	MM 67	80	53
Knappertsbusch[a] BPO/1951	MM 57	82	53
Furtwängler[a] VPO/1954	MM 54	60	42
Schuricht[c] VPO/1964	MM 70	76	49
Jochum[c] BPO/1964	MM 70	75	53
Böhm[c] VPO/1977	MM 70	55	48
Masur[b] Gewandhaus/1978	MM 55	52	47
Barenboim[b] CSO/1981	MM 55	60	40
Giulini[c] VPO/1984	MM 50	51	37
Karajan[b] VPO/1988	MM 63	55	49
Maazel[c] BPO/1989	MM 57	43	48
Eichhorn[c] Linz/1991	MM 62	60	41

Table 6.3 (*cont.*)

	mm. 583–90	mm. 609–16	mm. 637–40
Lopez–Cobos[c] Cincinnati/1993	MM 61	57	45
Wand[b] NGRSO/1993	MM 57	51	40
Dohnanyi[b] Cleveland/1994	MM 61	62	43

The measure numbers follow the Nowak edition. The three excerpts correspond to mm. 617–26, 651–6, and 675–80 of the Haas edition.

[a] 1892 edition
[b] Haas edition
[c] 1890 version, ed. Nowak

Knappertsbusch (1888–1965) naturally exemplify this approach, but other conductors of the old school, notably Carl Schuricht (1880–1967), Wilhelm Furtwängler (1886–1954), and Eugen Jochum (1902–87), played this passage in the spirit of the 1892 version no matter what edition they were actually using. Recordings from the 1980s and 1990s by such eminent figures as Karajan (1908–89), Günter Wand (b. 1912), Carlo Maria Giulini (b. 1914), and Lorin Maazel (b. 1930) present this music much differently; as a rule, these performances set a rather broader basic tempo (perhaps reflecting Nowak's "viel langsamer" in m. 583), abstain from dramatic tempo fluctuations – especially increases – and place great store by fullness of tone, precise ensemble, and textural clarity. (Barenboim's tempi reflect something of the older tradition.)

Differing performances of the re-appearance of the main theme of the first movement (mm. 617–23), an obvious high-point, encapsulate the evolution in interpretive approaches. The 1892 edition (and most older conductors) highlights this moment by surging through it as the crest of a wave. The modern tendency is to approach this point with steady, inexorable strides and during the statement itself allow the weighty brass tone ample time to resound; indeed, most current-day conductors broaden the tempo – not hasten it – at this spot. Today we usually hear this passage unfold patiently and splendidly; older generations of listeners, likely reaching back to the 1890s, heard it played as high musical drama.[32]

These developments in performance style obviously parallel the rise of the "Urtext" editions of Haas and Nowak, yet the sea change that Bruckner performance experienced in the third quarter of the twentieth century was not based solely on the emerging supremacy of modern editions. During this era, performance styles in general moved in the same general directions traceable in the evolution of Bruckner performances: performers began to favor steadier tempi, to eschew marked accelerandi, and generally to pursue interpretive sobriety and "objectivity." This impulse to play simply "what is written" ("com'è scritto" in Toscanini's famous words) is often justified as simple adherence to a composer's intentions, and as the renunciation of overly personal, subjective, or "romantic" approaches to interpretations. With the Bruckner Eighth, as we have seen, this position rests on slippery historical and text-critical ground, and in any case, pinning down a composer's intentions about performance (or about anything else, for that matter) is always a tricky business – or, better, an endlessly fascinating project. Surely it is unwise, and perhaps obfuscatory, to claim that this score or that score preserves in amber "Bruckner's interpretation."[33] Furthermore, framing the question in terms of narrowly defined notions of authorial intention is not the most enlightening approach. Performance styles, changing standards of scholarship, the evolving meaning of a given repertory, and the ideological, social, and material foundations of musical culture exist in a complex interrelationship. The overtly dramatic interpretations of Bruckner's symphonies of generations past were part of musical culture that differed crucially from ours. At that time a symphony was an event to be experienced in a concert hall, and conductors aimed to put the music across to the audience as vividly and persuasively as possible (an impulse nicely reflected in the 1892 score). Now, in an age of infinitely repeatable digital recordings, musicians are prone to be much more restrained. A recorded musical work is liable to be listened to in a living room (or even on headphones), heard repeatedly, and sometimes closely scrutinized, but more often attended to casually; as a result, listening to music, especially symphonic music, becomes less a rare transporting event than a matter of either relatively inattentive consumption or exquisite delectation.

Just as manners of performance contribute decisively to a work's aesthetic effect and its perceived meaning, at the same time they reflect changing attitudes toward the nature and significance of a given repertory. Walter and Furtwängler, for example, presented the sixty-odd measures before the coda of the Finale as an intense, viscerally affecting experience, more gripping and ultimately more cathartic than attractive. Half a century later, Wand, Giulini and Maazel played it serious, solemn, and beautiful. We can trace a parallel evolution in the metaphors used to describe Bruckner's music. Schalk's program notes from 1892 depict the titanic struggles of Prometheus. For Ernst Kurth (1886–1946), Bruckner's music was composed of great "symphonic waves" that play out musical energy through space and time. Furtwängler found "battles of demons [*Kämpfe der Dämonen*]" as well as "sounds of blessed transfiguration" in Bruckner's music.[34] Now it is far more common to concentrate descriptions of Bruckner's symphonies on images of peace and stability. Robert Simpson wrote, in a moving and resonant phrase, that "the essence of Bruckner's music lies in a patient search for pacification."[35] The close relationship of this attitude and the interpretive approach of most modern conductors is not hard to see; yet an attitude of reverent patience is prone to obscure other, rather different and deeply important qualities that may be found in Bruckner's music. Now it is easy to feel that the Eighth has become all too tame and has lost much of the urgent excitement and demonic struggle that emerged from it a century, or even half a century, ago. Studying the symphony in its 1892 edition may open new corridors for interpretation and perhaps help provide us with a renewed purchase on the work's awesome vitality and its visionary, even apocalyptic, quest for deliverance. For this reason, if no other, this score surely deserves serious attention and – is it too much to hope? – the passionate creative energies of modern-day conductors.

Appendix A

Haas's edition of the Eighth Symphony

Robert Haas's edition of the Eighth Symphony is a problem. It was one of the last of his Bruckner editions to appear, and it represents his editorial approach at its most extreme. Despite its label of "Original Version," Haas's edition does not strictly follow either the 1887 version or the 1890 version, but instead is an editorial conflation that incorporates some elements derived from the 1887 version into the text of the 1890 version. Haas justified this procedure on the basis of what he understood to be the story of the symphony's creation and revision. He believed that Bruckner was crushed by Levi's response to the 1887 version and contended that in its aftermath Bruckner was subject to manipulation, if not coercion, by Levi and Josef Schalk. In the preface to his score, Haas wrote darkly of Bruckner's "forced promise [*abgezwungene Versprechen*]" to revise the symphony and of the "coerced cuts [*abgenötige Kürzungen*]" found in the revised version. Because of this supposed taint of external influence (what Haas called "fremden Einflußbereichs"), Haas felt called upon when preparing his edition, which is based primarily on the 1890 version, to "reach back to the first version in some passages, in order to restore the authentic sound and sense."[1]

Compared to the 1890 version, Haas's score contains sporadic minor changes in the orchestration, which are derived from the 1887 version, in the first movement, the Finale, and more extensive ones in the Adagio. (He made no such alterations in the Scherzo.) The form of the first two movements was left intact, but in the two final movements Haas selectively "undid" some of the cuts Bruckner had made in the course of his revision. Haas believed that the cuts that Bruckner effected by simply crossing out passages reflected a "nonchalant manner of revision" and were made without the composer's "inner participation," and thus were not legitimate. (This despite the fact that all the revisions are confirmed by Bruckner's characteristic "metrical numbers," which demonstrate that the composer did consider them seriously.[2]) Accordingly, Haas's edition contains several sections from the 1887 version that Bruckner struck from the 1890 version: in the Adagio a stretch of ten measures is reinstated following m. 208 (mm. 209–18 in Haas's score), and in the Finale, mm. 211–14 of the 1890 text are replaced by twenty measures from the first version, four bars are reinstated following m. 238 of the 1890 version, twelve bars are restored following m. 566 of the 1890 version, and four bars following m. 636 of the 1890 version (these are mm. 211–30, 255–8, 587–98, and 671–4, respectively, in Haas's score). Haas also replaced mm. 577–82 of the 1890 version with a new eight-bar passage (mm. 609–16 in Haas's score). (Haas seems to have synthesized this passage himself by composing out the underlying harmonies of the 1887 version of this passage to fit a sketchy flute part Bruckner penciled into the upper margin of the revised manuscript. All of the material Haas worked with was clearly deleted by Bruckner and obviously replaced.) This creative editing surely exceeds reasonable limits of scholarly responsibility; moreover, his edition does not include any scholarly apparatus nor does the introduction adequately explain this editorial intervention.[3]

Haas's motivations are obscure. Presumably he came to feel that he was able to identify so strongly with Bruckner that he could intuit the composer's true intentions even though there is no actual evidence that Bruckner's revision involved any coercion, manipulation, or hastiness and nonchalance. It is hard to ignore the consanguinity of Haas's approach and the cultural politics of National Socialism. Haas's portentous rhetoric about Bruckner and "greater Germany" surely evokes the passions of the time (as is acutely evident in his comments quoted in Chapter 1) and his stated mission finally to "liberate the true symphonic will of the Master" seems to embody something of the Nazi ethic.[4] Whatever Haas's thought process, it is paradoxical that a scholar who railed so fiercely against what he perceived as the illegitimate and intrusive editorial practices of the Schalk brothers and Ferdinand Löwe should himself intervene editorially in such extreme and obviously unauthorized ways.

Although the Haas edition is now obtainable only as a photo-reprint study score, a number of prominent conductors – including Bernard

Haitink, Günter Wand, Herbert von Karajan, and Daniel Barenboim – committed themselves to this version of the symphony.[5] Several writers, including Robert Simpson and Deryck Cooke, have argued that Haas's score is musically superior to Nowak's. This point is of course debatable; it could be argued, for example, that the passage Haas inserted in the Adagio unnecessarily dissipates the accumulating tension that spans much of the final third of the movement. In the end, however one might respond to Haas's edition, it must not be forgotten that it does not correspond to any version of the symphony that Bruckner actually wrote.

Appendix B

Textual differences between the Finale in the 1890 version and the 1892 edition

The musical text of the 1892 edition is currently almost unknown. It does, nevertheless, have a very negative reputation. Deryck Cooke, for example, called it "an appalling picture of the muddled, amateurish and senseless desecration. . . brought about by his pupils' tampering."[1] Such dismissive description is not only tendentious, but it is also seriously in error. For this reason, it seems worthwhile to tabulate its differences from Nowak's well-known and authoritative edition of the 1890 version. The Finale contains the most important and numerous points of variance, and thus can serve as a representative example of the whole. This list is not exhaustive, but it does contain all significant textual differences. (Changes to the dynamics are not noted, but also see p. 94 above.)

Changes in orchestration
(measure numbers follow the 1890 version)

m. 56	"loco" missing from Wagner tuba I; thus mm. 56–65 are played in the lower octave. (This is likely a misprint.)
mm. 93–8	these bars are cut
mm. 101–3 and 107–9	Cl. added doubling Hn.
mm. 123–4	Vc. and Cb. play pizzicato
mm. 159–66	Vn. I and II muted
mm. 163–66	muted, divided Vc. added
mm. 304–7	Vn. I divided in octaves
mm. 331–2	4 Hn. added to the bass line ($f'/g\flat'/g'/a'$)

mm. 334, 338, and 342	quarter-note rests inserted in Trpt. and Tbn.
mm. 337–8	some rests inserted in Fl., Ob., Cl., Hn.
mm. 341–2	some rests inserted in Fl., Ob., Cl., Hn.
mm. 343–5	Trpt. III removed
mm. 379–84	repeated-note figure continues in Hn.
mm. 381/83–4	Cl. added
m. 385	last note of Ob. I is a♭″ not e♭‴
mm. 399–400	three Hn. hold their notes through these bars
mm. 437–62	timpani part elaborated
m. 479	cymbal crash added
mm. 493–6	off-beat answers played by Hn., not Trpt.
mm. 501–3	Trpt. III slightly altered
following m. 520	two bars added (they repeat the two preceding bars)
mm. 601–6	Vla. play tremolando
mm. 609–16	Vc. play pizzicato
mm. 613–16	Fl. added to Ob./Cl. chords
mm. 627–30	tremolando Vc. and Vla. added
mm. 635–7	Vc. play tremolando/Fl. *ff* (not *f*)
mm. 637–40	Ob./Cl./Hn. play (not Vn. I, Vla.)/Vn. II plays tremolando/< > added
mm. 641–2	Wagner tubas play (not Vn. I and II, Vla. and Vc.)
mm. 641–3	Cl. added to Fl.
mm. 688–90	Ob. and Cl. double Trpt. fanfares
mm. 691–6	Fl., Ob., and Cl. double Trpt. fanfares
mm. 697–709	Hn. III and IV altered

Added tempo and expression markings

mm. 101–3 and mm. 107–9	< > added to Cl. and Hn.
m. 183	"Erstes Zeitmass" added
m. 206	"poco accel." added
mm. 208–9	"rit."/"a tempo" added
mm. 221–3	"etwas zurückhaltend"/"a tempo" added
mm. 221–3	"etwas zurückhaltend"/"a tempo (ruhig)" added
m. 239	"betont" added to Fl.
m. 250	"ruhig" added
m. 265	"mit ruhigen, gesangvollen Vortrage" added/ the articulation in the strings is a bit different
m. 279	"ekstatisch bewegt" added to Vn.
m. 291	"bewegt, doch nicht eilend" added
m. 297	"nachlassend" added
m. 317	"nach und nach wieder belebter" added
m. 323	"ziemlich lebhaft" added
m. 331	"molto cresc" added
mm. 385–6	"dim. e ritard." added
mm. 428–9	"rit."/"a tempo" added
m. 468–72	these bars alternate between "sehr breit 4/4" and "a tempo (2/2)"
mm. 473–5	"belebend bis – – – a tempo (2/2)" added
m. 480	"molto rit." added
m. 481	"a tempo (ruhig)" added
m. 577	Hn. and Wagner tubas are silent
m. 583	"sehr ruhig beginnend" (not "viel langsam")
m. 593	"sehr allmählich belebend" added
m. 601	"poco a poco cresc. ed accelerando" added
m. 609	"accel." added

m. 617	"Lebhaft" added
m. 622	"zurückhaltend" (not "langsam")
m. 626	"zurückhaltend" added
m. 627	"und immer ruhiger werdend" added
m. 647	"G.P." added to this bar of rest
mm. 679	"Erstes Zeitmass" added
m. 704	"Ein wenig beschleunigend" added

Notes

Introduction

1 August Göllerich and Max Auer, *Anton Bruckner: Ein Lebens- und Schaffens-bild*, 4 vols. in 9 parts (Regensburg, 1922–37), IV/3, 21.

2 I allude to Walter Wiora's well-known essay "Zwischen absoluter und Pro-grammusik" in *Festschrift Friedrich Blume zum 70. Geburtstag*, ed. Anna Amalie Abert and Wilhelm Pfannkuch (Kassel, 1963), 381–8.

3 William Rothstein, *Phrase Rhythm in Tonal Music* (New York, 1989), 249.

1 Placing the Eighth Symphony

1 See Bekker's *Die Sinfonie von Beethoven bis Mahler* (Berlin, 1918). Also see Margaret Notley, "*Volksconcerte* in Vienna and Late-Nineteenth Century Ideology of the Symphony," *Journal of the American Musicological Society* 50 (1997), 421–53 and Stephen Hinton, "Not *Which* Tones? The Crux of Beethoven's Ninth," *19th-Century Music* 22 (1998), 75, note 48.

2 Three previous subscription concerts had included a symphony by Bruck-ner: the Seventh Symphony on 21 March 1886, the Third on 21 December 1890, and the First on 13 December 1891, all under Richter. Otto Jahn had included the Adagio and Scherzo of the Sixth Symphony at a subscription concert on 11 February 1883. The Philharmonic also performed Bruckner symphonies at concerts sponsored by the Wiener akademischer Wagner-Verein (the Fourth was given on 20 February 1881, the Seventh on 24 Febru-ary 1889, and the Third on 25 January 1891). Another performance of the Fourth on 22 January 1888 was also privately funded.

3 See August Göllerich and Max Auer, *Anton Bruckner: Ein Lebens- und Schaffensbild*, 4 vols. in 9 parts (Regensburg, 1922–37), IV/3, 284–5.

4 See Clemens Hellsberg, *Demokratie der Könige: Die Geschichte der Wiener Philharmoniker* (Vienna, 1992), 275.

5 Review dated 5 January 1893, excerpted in Norbert Tschulik, *Bruckner im*

Spiegel seiner Zeit (Vienna, 1955), 51. Unless otherwise noted all translations are by the author.

6 "-n.," review dated 21 December 1892 in *Das Vaterland*, rpt. in Franz Grasberger, "Das Bruckner-Bild der Zeitung 'Das Vaterland' in den Jahren 1870–1900" in *Festschrift Hans Schneider zum 60. Geburtstag*, ed. Rudolf Elvers and Ernst Vogel (Munich, 1981), 126 (emphasis in the original).

7 Review of Bruckner's Eighth Symphony, *Neue Freie Presse*, 23 December 1892; rpt. in Eduard Hanslick, *Fünf Jahre Musik* (Berlin, 1899), 190–1; English trans. in Eduard Hanslick, *Music Criticisms 1846–99*, trans. Henry Pleasants (Baltimore, 1950), 288–9, translation modified.

8 See the photo of the leaflet in Hans-Hubert Schönzeler, *Bruckner* (London, 1970), 158.

9 Göllerich and Auer, *Anton Bruckner*, IV/3, 298.

10 *Oesterreichische Volks-Zeitung*, 21 December 1892; quoted in Manfred Wagner, "Zur Rezeptionsgeschichte von Anton Bruckners Achter Symphonie," *Bruckner Jahrbuch 1991/92/93* (Linz, 1995), 115.

11 Rpt. in Grasberger, "Das Bruckner-Bild der Zeitung 'Das Vaterland,' " 128.

12 Quoted in Wagner, "Zur Rezeptionsgeschichte," 111; also see Ingrid Fuchs in "Round Table: Bruckner und die österreichische Presse" in *Bruckner-Symposion: Bruckner Rezeption*, ed. Othmar Wessely (Linz, 1991), 91, note 43.

13 Letter to Emil Kauffmann, 23 December 1892 in *Hugo Wolf's Briefe an Emil Kauffmann*, ed. Edmund Heller (Berlin, 1903), 82.

14 Karl Grunsky, *Anton Bruckner* (Stuttgart, 1922), 86–7. Franz Gräflinger also analogized with Goethe's *Faust*; see "Bruckners Achte Sinfonie" in *In Memoriam Anton Bruckner*, ed. Karl Kobald (Vienna, 1924), 100–13, esp. p. 113.

15 Heinrich Schenker, "Anton Bruckner," *Die Zeit* 7 (1896); rpt. in Schenker, *Heinrich Schenker als Essayist und Kritiker: gesammelte Aufsätze, Rezensionen und kleinere Berichte aus den Jahren 1891–1901*, ed. Hellmut Federhofer (Hildesheim, 1990), 200–1.

16 Ibid., 202.

17 Ibid., 203–4.

18 Kurth, *Bruckner* (Berlin, 1925), 1035–99; also see 346–55.

19 Leichtentritt, *Musikalische Formenlehre*, 3rd edn. (Leipzig, 1927), 384–426; English trans., *Musical Form* (Cambridge, Mass., 1961), 379–424.

20 See Leopold Nowak, "Die Anton Bruckner-Gesamtausgabe: Ihre Geschichte und Schicksale" in *Bruckner Jahrbuch 1982/83* (Linz, 1984), 33–67 and Benjamin Korstvedt, "'Return to the Pure Sources': The Ideology and Text-Critical Legacy of the First Bruckner *Gesamtausgabe*" in

Bruckner Studies, ed. Timothy Jackson and Paul Hawkshaw (Cambridge, 1997), 91–109.

21 Robert Haas, "Einführung" in *Anton Bruckner Sämtliche Werke, 8. Band: VIII. Symphonie C-Moll (Originalfassung), Studienpartitur*, ed. Haas (Leipzig, 1939). Haas generally toned down his comments in the 1949 reprint of the score, and entirely removed the allusion to the political significance of the symphony.

22 On the relationship of postwar and Nazi-era Bruckner reception, see Korstvedt, "Anton Bruckner in the Third Reich and After: an Essay on Ideology and Bruckner Reception," *Musical Quarterly* 80 (1996), 132–60.

23 Theodor Adorno, "Alienated Masterpiece: the *Missa Solemnis* (1959)," trans. Duncan Smith, *Telos* 28 (1976), 113.

2 The genesis and evolution of the Eighth Symphony

1 Claudia Röthig, *Studien zur Systematik des Schaffens von Anton Bruckner* (Göttingen, 1978), 234.

2 Thomas Leibnitz, *Die Brüder Schalk und Anton Bruckner* (Tutzing, 1988), 72.

3 Anton Bruckner, *Gesammelte Briefe*, neue Folge, ed. Max Auer (Regensburg, 1924), 194; Bruckner, *Gesammelte Briefe*, ed. Franz Gräflinger (Regensburg, 1924), 194, 92; Steffen Lieberwirth, "Anton Bruckner und Leipzig: Einige neue Erkenntnisse und Ergänzungen," *Bruckner Jahrbuch 1989/90* (Linz, 1992), 283–4.

4 See the transcriptions in August Göllerich and Max Auer, *Anton Bruckner: Ein Lebens- und Schaffensbild*, 4 vols. in 9 parts (Regensburg, 1922–37), IV/2, 543–6 and in Röthig, *Studien zur Systematik*, 342–3.

5 A-Wn Mus. Hs. 6070; see the facsimile in Franz Grasberger, *Anton Bruckner zum 150. Geburtstag (eine Ausstellung)* (Vienna, 1974), 3.

6 See Leibnitz, *Die Brüder Schalk und Anton Bruckner*, 102 and Franz Schalk, *Briefe und Betrachtungen*, ed. Lili Schalk (Vienna, 1935), 70.

7 Very few sketches exist for any of Bruckner's works other than the two final symphonies, for which they exist copiously. Many earlier compositional materials were destroyed by Bruckner in 1895 as he prepared to move from his long-established apartment on Heßgasse to his final residence, the Kustodenstöckl of Schloß Belvedere; see Göllerich and Auer, *Anton Bruckner*, IV/3, 521.

8 The sketches are preserved as A-Wn Mus. Hs. 6052; see Röthig, *Studien zur Systematik*, 339.

9 On date of the relocation of the Adagio, see Röthig, *Studien zur Systematik*,

234 and Franz Scheder, *Anton Bruckner Chronologie*, 2 vols. (Tutzing, 1996), I, 511 and 514.

10 Gräflinger, *Anton Bruckner: Leben und Schaffen (Umgearbeitete Bausteine)* (Berlin, 1927), 334.

11 Göllerich and Auer, *Anton Bruckner*, IV/3, 537.

12 Bruckner's original manuscript of the 1887 version is not preserved in its original state. The first three movements do remain in their original form in the Musiksammlung of the Österreichische Nationalbibliothek: the two opening movements are A-Wn Mus. Hs. 6083 and 6084, respectively, and Bruckner's 1887 manuscript of the Adagio is now preserved as the third volume of A-Wn Mus. Hs. 19.840, which otherwise contains the 1890 version. Bruckner used his 1887 autograph of the Finale as the basis for his later revision of the movement (now preserved as volume IV of A-Wn Mus. Hs. 19.840), thereby obscuring much of the initial text. The 1887 version of this movement can only be recovered from Aigner's copy (A-Wn Mus. Hs. 6001). See Nowak's preface in *Anton Bruckner Sämtliche Werke, Band VIII/1: VIII. Symphonie C-moll, Fassung von 1887* (Vienna, 1972) and Dermot Gault, "For Later Times," *Musical Times* 137 (1996), 16.

13 It is likely that Bruckner had more than one copy of the score made; not only was this his usual practice, but although no other complete copy now exists, several fragments do.

14 Gräflinger, *Anton Bruckner*, 338.

15 Ibid., 339.

16 Max Auer wrote, for example, that the time Bruckner spent revising the Eighth Symphony "was the real reason . . . that work on the Ninth Symphony was postponed" and was why that work "remained a torso"; *Anton Bruckner: Sein Leben und Werk* (Vienna, 1947), 409.

17 Letter of 30 November 1884; Gräflinger, *Anton Bruckner*, 338 and Frithjof Haas, *Zwischen Brahms und Wagner: der Dirigent Hermann Levi* (Zurich, 1995), 299.

18 On these events in Munich, see Haas, *Zwischen Brahms und Wagner*, 300–2.

19 See Göllerich and Auer, *Anton Bruckner*, IV/2, 486–90.

20 On the events that led to the award see Brigitte Hamann, "Musikalisches aus dem Tagebuch der Prinzessin Amélie in Bayern," in *Bruckner-Symposion 1994: Bruckner-Freunde, Bruckner-Kenner* (Linz, 1997), 21–3.

21 Gräflinger, *Anton Bruckner*, 333.

22 Göllerich and Auer, *Anton Bruckner*, IV/3, 181–2.

23 See Bruckner's letters to Levi dated 8 December 1884 and 3 January 1887 in Gräflinger, *Anton Bruckner*, 326 and 335.

24 Letter dated 30 September 1887; *Briefe*, ed. Auer, 395; Göllerich and Auer, *Anton Bruckner*, IV/2, 560–1; Leibnitz, *Die Brüder Schalk und Anton Bruckner*, 130–1.

25 The letter is in the Bayerische Staatsbibliothek (Munich), Leviana. Excerpts are included in Haas, *Zwischen Brahms und Wagner*, 306 and 379.

26 This translation is by Laurence Dreyfus, to whom I am indebted for generously sharing his discovery with me.

27 *Briefe*, ed. Auer, 396; Göllerich and Auer, *Anton Bruckner*, IV/2, 562; Leibnitz, *Die Brüder Schalk und Anton Bruckner*, 131.

28 Haas, "Vorlagenbericht" in *Anton Bruckner Sämtliche Werke, 4. Band/1. Teil: IV. Symphonie Es–Dur (Fassung von 1878 mit dem Finale von 1880), Finale von 1878, Partituren und Entwürfe mit Bericht* (Vienna, 1936), II.

29 Letter of 20 October 1887 in Gräflinger, *Anton Bruckner*, 339; Göllerich and Auer, *Anton Bruckner*, IV/2, 563. Bruckner mentioned his idea of organizing a reading of the symphony, with Levi present, at his expense to Princess Amélie on 23 October; see Hamann, "Musikalisches aus dem Tagebuch," 25.

30 Hamann, "Musikalisches aus dem Tagebuch," 25.

31 Bruckner noted the date 3 December 1887 in a score of the Finale (A-Wn Mus.Hs. 6047), although he seems not to have made any changes at this time; see Röthig, *Studien zur Systematik*, 235–6.

32 *Briefe*, ed. Auer, 220.

33 Gräflinger, *Anton Bruckner*, 341.

34 Bruckner worked with a copy of the score prepared in 1887 by Hofmeyer. In the process of revisions Bruckner replaced numerous pages with new ones written in his own hand. This manuscript entered the collection of the ÖNB only in 1990 (A-Wn Mus. Hs. 4099); see Günter Brosche, "Quellen für künftige Forschungen," *Studien zur Musikwissenschaft* (1993), 425–6. Gault reports that an intermediate version of the Adagio is preserved in yet another copyist's score (A-Wn Mus. Hs. 34.614); see "For Later Times," 16.

35 A-Wn Mus. Hs. 19.480, vol. IV.

36 A-Wn Mus. Hs. 19.480, vol. II.

37 A-Wn Mus. Hs. 19.480, vol. I.

38 Bruckner's prayer list of 15 March: "14.3.90 letzte auswendige Wiederholung v. I. Satze der 8. Sinf."; see Göllerich and Auer, *Anton Bruckner*, IV/3, 124 and Leopold Nowak, "Anton Bruckners Achte Symphonie und ihre zweite Fassung" in *Über Anton Bruckner* (Vienna, 1985), 27.

39 The copying was done in the winter of 1889–90 by Leopold Hofmeyer and Victor Christ. See Erich Partsch, "Bruckner-Pflege in Steyr bis zur

Jahrhundertwende," *Mitteilungsblatt der Internationalen Bruckner-Gesellschaft* 35 (1990), 5–6 and Andrea Harrandt, "Unbekannte Bruckner-Autographe entdeckt," *Österreichische Musikzeitschrift* 49 (1994), 32.

40 Gräflinger, *Anton Bruckner*, 338.

41 March 1890; *Briefe*, ed. Auer, 229; Göllerich and Auer, *Anton Bruckner*, IV/3, 46; Manfred Wagner, *Anton Bruckner* (Mainz, 1983), 291.

42 Max von Oberleithner, *Meine Erinnerungen an Anton Bruckner* (Regensburg, 1933), 52 and Gräflinger, *Anton Bruckner*, 342.

43 Schalk, *Briefe und Betrachtungen*, 52.

44 See Korstvedt, "The First Edition of Anton Bruckner's Fourth Symphony: Authorship, Production, and Reception" (Ph.D. diss., University of Pennsylvania, 1995), 315–16.

45 Göllerich and Auer, *Anton Bruckner*, IV/3, 48–9.

46 Gräflinger, *Anton Bruckner*, 342.

47 See his letter of 27 March 1891 to Weingartner in *Briefe*, ed. Gräflinger, 131–2 and *Briefe*, ed. Auer, 241 (dated incorrectly as 17 March 1891). On 15 June 1891 Siegfried Ochs wrote to Bruckner that the Berlin firm Raabe und Plotow was willing to publish the Eighth Symphony, including piano scores, for a fee of 1,200 florins; see *Briefe*, ed. Auer, 341 and Göllerich and Auer, *Anton Bruckner*, IV/3, 162. By this time Bruckner had already reached an agreement with Haslinger, and wrote to Ochs that he would keep Raabe in reserve; see letter dated 15 June 1891 in *Briefe*, ed. Auer, 249–50; *Briefe*, ed. Gräflinger, 94–5; Göllerich and Auer, *Anton Bruckner*, IV/3, 163–4.

48 Oberleithner, *Erinnerungen*, 52–3.

49 Ibid., 53.

50 When he was preparing to perform the Seventh Symphony in Leipzig in 1884 Nikisch, for example, avoided presenting the work as part of the Gewandhaus subscription concerts so as to minimize the antagonism of Leipzig's traditionalists; instead it was given as part of the "Opern-Abonnement" at the Neues Theater. See Steffen Lieberwirth, *Anton Bruckner und Leipzig: Die Jahre 1884–1902*, Anton Bruckner Dokumente und Studien 6 (Graz, 1988), 18–26, 42.

51 Letter of 7 October 1887; see note 27 above.

52 Bayerische Staatsbibliothek (Munich), Leviana, courtesy of Laurence Dreyfus.

53 20 September 1890; *Briefe*, ed. Auer, 320–1.

54 2 October 1890; *Briefe*, ed. Auer, 233.

55 *Briefe*, ed. Auer, 368–9.

56 Ibid., 369–70.

57 8 April 1891; Bayerische Staatsbibliothek (Munich), Leviana, courtesy of Laurence Dreyfus.

58 Gräflinger, *Anton Bruckner*, 347–8; Göllerich and Auer, *Anton Bruckner*, IV/3, 143.

59 *Briefe*, ed. Auer, 369–70.

60 Ibid., 233; *Briefe*, ed. Gräflinger, 129.

61 Gault, "For Later Times," 18.

62 *Briefe*, ed. Auer, 237.

63 Ibid., 241 (dated 17 March); *Briefe*, ed. Gräflinger, 131–2.

64 See for example Haas, "Einführung" in *Anton Bruckner Sämtliche Werke, 2. Band: II. Symphonie C-moll, Studienpartitur* (Vienna, 1938).

65 See Göllerich and Auer, *Anton Bruckner*, IV/3, 73. Bruckner always used copy scores, not his precious autograph manuscripts (which would in any case have been very difficult to read on the podium), for performances.

66 Gräflinger, *Anton Bruckner*, 352.

67 Ibid., 353.

68 Bruckner reported Levi's plans in a letter to Weingartner dated 8 August 1891 (see *Briefe*, ed. Auer, 250; *Briefe*, ed. Gräflinger, 132–3) and a letter to Ludwig Koch von Langetreu dated 27 July 1892 (*Briefe*, ed. Auer, 259–60; *Briefe*, ed. Gräflinger, 33–4).

69 Scheder, *Bruckner Chronologie*, vol. I, 685.

70 *Briefe*, ed. Auer, 326.

71 Quoted in Leibnitz, *Die Brüder Schalk und Anton Bruckner*, 166.

3 The musical design and symphonic agenda of the Eighth

1 On symphonic monumentality see Norbert Nägler, "Bruckners gründerzeitliche Monumentalsymphonie," *Musik-Konzepte 23/24: Anton Bruckner* (Munich, 1982), 86–118, esp. 109–13; and Margaret Notley, "*Volksconcerte* in Vienna and Late Nineteenth-Century Ideology of the Symphony," *Journal of the American Musicological Society* 50 (1997), 432–9.

2 Letter to Max Marschalk, 26 March 1896, quoted and trans. in Peter Franklin, *Mahler: Symphony no. 3* (Cambridge, 1991), 15.

3 Nägler, "Bruckners gründerzeitliche Monumentalsymphonie," 112.

4 Bloch, *Essays in the Philosophy of Music*, trans. Peter Palmer (Cambridge, 1985), 42–3. Also see Carl Dahlhaus, *The Idea of Absolute Music*, trans. Roger Lustig (Chicago, 1989), 122–3.

5 See Dahlhaus, "Wagner's Musical Influence" in *The Wagner Handbook*, ed. Ulrich Müller and Peter Wapnewski, translation ed. John Deathridge (Cambridge, Mass., 1992), 553.

6 See Carl Dahlhaus's important discussion of the relationship of harmonic style and formal design during the period in "Issues in Composition" in

Between Romanticism and Modernism, trans. Mary Whittall (Berkeley and Los Angeles, 1980), 40–78.

7　Arnold Schoenberg, *Structural Functions of Harmony*, rev. edn. (New York, 1969), 3.

8　Ibid., 3 and 164–5.

9　Werner Korte, *Bruckner und Brahms: Die spätromantische Lösung der autonomen Konzeption* (Tutzing, 1963), 25.

10　Carl Dahlhaus, "Bruckner und die Programmusik: zum Finale der Achten Symphonie" in *Anton Bruckner: Studien zu Werk und Wirkung, Walter Wiora zum 30. Dezember 1986* (Tutzing, 1988), 23. Also see Dahlhaus, *Nineteenth-Century Music*, trans. J. Bradford Robinson (Berkeley and Los Angeles, 1989), 272–4.

11　See Korte, *Bruckner und Brahms*, esp. 24–9, 34–8, 44–57; Paul Dawson-Bowling, "Thematic and Tonal Unity in Bruckner's Eighth Symphony," *Music Review* 30 (1969), 225–36, and Erwin Horn, "Evolution und Metamorphose in der Achten Symphonie von Anton Bruckner: Darstellung der thematischen Zusammenhänge," *Bruckner Jahrbuch 1989/90* (Linz, 1992), 7–34.

12　"Über die Anwendung der Musik auf das Drama" (1879), quoted and trans. in Carl Dahlhaus, "The Music" in *The Wagner Handbook*, 304.

13　Critics and analysts have not agreed on where the recapitulation begins. Some writers have placed it at m. 225; see Robert Simpson, *The Essence of Bruckner*, rev. edn. (London, 1992), 194–5; Erwin Doernberg, *The Life and Symphonies of Anton Bruckner* (London, 1960), 197. A larger group have located it at m. 283; see Alfred Orel, *Anton Bruckner: Das Werk, der Künstler, die Zeit* (Vienna, 1925), 85; Robert Haas, *Anton Bruckner* (Potsdam, 1934), 147; Hugo Leichtentritt, *Musical Form* (Cambridge, Mass., 1961), 386; Constantin Floros, "Die Fassungen der Achten Symphonie von Anton Bruckner" in *Bruckner-Symposion: Die Fassungen*, ed. Franz Grasberger (Linz, 1981), 55–6; and Willibald Kähler, "Sinfonie No. VIII (C moll)" in *Bruckner's Symphonien*, Meisterführer Nr. 4, ed. Karl Grunsky (Berlin and Vienna, n.d. [1907]), 157–8. As ever, Ernst Kurth refused to cut and dry things, *Bruckner* (Berlin, 1925), 1044–7.

14　Eckstein, *"Alte unnennbare Tage!"* (Vienna, 1936), 145.

15　Brinkmann, *Late Idyll: The Second Symphony of Johannes Brahms*, trans. Peter Palmer (Cambridge, Mass., 1995), 144.

16　The one important exception is the second movement of the Fourth Symphony, which is marked "Andante quasi Allegretto."

17　Bruckner began sketching the Adagio very shortly after he attended a performance of *Tristan* in Leipzig on 27 December 1884 (the earliest extant sketches of the Adagio are from the following month). Bruckner also apparently returned to the score of this movement after he heard *Tristan* in Bayreuth in late July 1886 (see Franz Scheder, *Anton Bruckner Chronologie*, 2 vols. [Tutzing, 1996], I, 510–11).

18   August Göllerich and Max Auer, *Anton Bruckner: Ein Lebens- und Schaffensbild*, 4 vols. in 9 parts (Regensburg, 1936), IV/3, 19.

19   This tune is strongly prefigured in Bruckner's "Fantasie" for piano of 1868 (WAB 118), mm. 13–16. (I thank Bill Carragan for pointing this out to me.)

20   See Kurth, *Bruckner*, 1066–8.

21   On the "Finale Problem" see Paul Bekker, *Gustav Mahlers Sinfonien* (Berlin, 1921), 15–20 and Brinkmann, *Late Idyll*, 203–17.

22   See Bruckner's letter to Franz Schalk, 16 August 1885; quoted in Thomas Leibnitz, *Die Brüder Schalk und Anton Bruckner* (Tutzing, 1988), 102.

23   Kurth, *Bruckner*, 1087.

24   For competing views on the nature and significance of this passage see Constantin Floros, *Brahms und Bruckner: Studien zur Musikalischen Exegetik* (Wiesbaden, 1980), 204–5, who emphasized its meaningful strangeness, and Dahlhaus, "Bruckner und die Programmusik," 23–4, who emphasized its explicability.

25   Simpson, *The Essence of Bruckner*, 209.

26   Derek Scott, "Bruckner and the Dialectic of Darkness and Light (II)," *Bruckner Journal 2/2* (1998), 13.

27   Simpson, *The Essence of Bruckner*, 232.

28   Scott, "Bruckner and the Dialectic of Darkness and Light," 12.

29   The full text of the program is in Göllerich and Auer, *Anton Bruckner*, IV/3, 288–90 and Leibnitz, *Die Brüder Schalk und Anton Bruckner*, 170–2.

30   Schalk's program contains two internal quotations. One is from Aeschylus, *Prometheus Bound*, lines 1041–52. The other is the opening lines, spoken by the Archangel Raphael, of the "Prologue in Heaven," in Goethe's *Faust*, lines 243–6.

31   See Hanslick's review in *Neue Freie Presse*, 23 December 1892; rpt. in Eduard Hanslick, *Fünf Jahre Musik* (Berlin, 1899), 190–1; English trans. in Eduard Hanslick, *Music Criticisms 1846–99*, trans. Henry Pleasants (Baltimore, 1950), 288–9 and Kalbeck's in the *Montags-Revue*, 19 December 1892; rpt. in Göllerich and Auer, *Anton Bruckner*, IV/3, 297–300. Even the favorable review of the symphony in *Das Vaterland*, 21 December 1892, commented negatively on Schalk's program; rpt. in Franz Grasberger, "Das Bruckner-Bild der Zeitung 'Das Vaterland' in den Jahren 1870–1900" in *Festschrift Hans Schneider zum 60. Geburtstag*, ed. Rudolf Elvers and Ernst

Vogel (Munich, 1981), 129. Hruby's comments can be found in *Bruckner Remembered*, ed. and trans. Stephen Johnson (London, 1998), 120.

32 See Kähler, "Symphonie No. VIII," 152–69 and Karl Grunsky, *Anton Bruckner* (Stuttgart, 1922), 87.

33 Dahlhaus, *The Idea of Absolute Music*, 135.

34 Quoted in Leibnitz, *Die Brüder Schalk und Anton Bruckner*, 237.

35 Letter of 27 January 1891, Anton Bruckner, *Gesammelte Briefe*, neue Folge, ed. Max Auer (Regensburg, 1924), 369–70; also see Floros, *Brahms und Bruckner*, 183.

36 Floros has argued that in this phrase Bruckner's handwriting is traditionally misread, and that the line actually reads: "finally it [i.e., Michael's tune] is plaintively inverted" ("endlich klagend kehrt es [not: er] selbes um"). This Floros suggests is a direct reference to mm. 95–8 of the Scherzo in which the main theme is inverted; see *Brahms und Bruckner*, 191 and 215.

37 In the 1980s the program provoked two significant, contrasting interpretations, Floros's *Brahms und Bruckner*, esp. 182–210, which entertains Bruckner's program seriously and Carl Dahlhaus's in "Bruckner und die Programmusik," which is rather less credulous.

38 On 14 January 1891 Hugo Wolf wrote that "Bruckner is (between us) enraged over the endless delay of his 8th, and recently I had great difficulty convincing him of Weingartner's sincerity and honest enthusiasm for his symphonies. He no longer believes in the performance in Mannheim"; quoted in Günter Brosche, "Anton Bruckner and Hugo Wolf" in *Bruckner Studien*, ed. Othmar Wessely (Vienna, 1975), 181.

39 See Kurth, *Bruckner*, 1048–9, note 1 and Hans Redlich, "Das programmatische Element bei Bruckner" in *Bruckner-Studien*, ed. Franz Grasberger (Vienna, 1964), 92–3.

40 See August Stradal, "Eine Erinnerung an Anton Bruckner," *Zeitschrift für Music* 93 (1926), 505–6 and "Erinnerungen aus Bruckners letzter Zeit," *Zeitschrift für Music* 99 (1932), 977, as well the comments recorded in Göllerich and Auer, *Anton Bruckner*, IV/3, 15–23. Bruckner explained to Theodor Helm that with his "Michel" theme he meant to depict "the German Austrians, not to jest"; quoted in ibid., IV/3, 16, note 1.

41 Quoted in Göllerich and Auer, *Anton Bruckner*, IV/3, 15. Bruckner used similar imagery in explaining this passage on other occasions, too; see Ernst Decsey, *Anton Bruckner* (Berlin, 1921), 216 and Eckstein, *"Alte unnennbare Tage"*, 145.

42 Korte, *Bruckner und Brahms*, 69.

43 Bruckner himself pointed out this evocation of Siegfried, which he said was

"in remembrance of the Master"; quoted in Göllerich and Auer, *Anton Bruckner*, IV/3, 19.

44 The significance of the first two of these examples is discussed in Floros, *Brahms und Bruckner*, 182–210, esp. 186 and 204–6 and Dahlhaus, "Bruckner und die Programmusik," esp. 12–13 and 22–26.

4 The Adagio and the sublime

1 Quoted in Thomas Leibnitz, *Die Brüder Schalk und Anton Bruckner* (Tutzing, 1988), 171.

2 Willibald Kähler, "Sinfonie No. VIII (C moll)" in *Bruckner's Sinfonien*, Meisterführer Nr. 4, ed. Karl Grunsky (Berlin and Vienna, n.d. [1907]), 165.

3 Engel, *The Symphonies of Anton Bruckner* (Iowa City, 1955), 70.

4 Edward Rothstein, "Contemplating the Sublime," *American Scholar* 66 (1997), 513.

5 Quoted in Dahlhaus, *The Idea of Absolute Music*, trans. Roger Lustig (Chicago, 1989), 59.

6 *Richard Wagner's Prose Works*, trans. William Ashton Ellis (London, 1896), vol. V, 93.

7 Brinkmann, *Late Idyll: The Second Symphony of Johannes Brahms*, trans. Peter Palmer (Cambridge, Mass., 1995), 202.

8 See, for example, Karl Grunsky's comments on the "truth" and "depth" that reside in the interior spaces of Bruckner's Adagios in *Anton Bruckner* (Stuttgart, 1922), 21–3.

9 Longinus, *On the Sublime*, trans. with commentary by James A. Arieti and John M. Crossett (New York, 1985).

10 Ibid., sec. 8.1, 46.

11 Ibid., sec. 9.2, 52–3. Also see Neil Hertz, "A Reading of Longinus" in *The End of the Line: Essays on Psychoanalysis and the Sublime* (New York, 1985), 1–20.

12 Longinus, *On the Sublime*, sec. 7.2, 42.

13 *On the Sublime* was rediscovered only in the sixteenth century, and its first important modern translation, by Boileau into French, appeared in 1674.

14 Simpson, "Commentary: Updating the Sublime," *Studies in Romanticism* 26 (1987), 245.

15 James Webster made a similar point in "The *Creation*, Haydn's Late Vocal Works, and the Musical Sublime" in *Haydn and his World*, ed. Elaine Sisman (Princeton, 1997), 60–1.

16 Elaine Sisman nicely explicated the rhetorical design of the Finale of Mozart's "Jupiter" Symphony, notably its use of the learned style as a "signifier of the sublime," *Mozart: The Jupiter Symphony* (Cambridge, 1993), 68–79, esp. 76.

17 On this renewed influence see, for example, "Longinus, Hazlitt, Keats, and the Criterion of Intensity" in M. H. Abrams, *The Mirror and the Lamp: Romantic Theory and the Critical Tradition* (New York, 1953), 132–8.

18 Edmund Burke, *A Philosophical Enquiry into the Origin of our Ideas of the Sublime and The Beautiful*, ed. James T. Boulton (Notre Dame, 1968).

19 Ibid., part III, section 1, p. 91.

20 Ibid, part I, section 7, p. 39.

21 The term "apprehensive synthesis" is Jean-François Lyotard's; see *Lessons on the Analytic of the Sublime*, trans. Elizabeth Rottenberg (Stanford, 1994), 81.

22 Kant, *Critique of Judgment*, trans. J. H. Bernhard (New York, 1951), §26, p. 94.

23 Monroe Beardsley, *Aesthetics from Classical Greece to the Present: A Short History* (New York, 1966; rpt., Tuscaloosa, Ala., 1975), 219.

24 Weiskel, *The Romantic Sublime: Studies in the Structure and Psychology of Transcendence* (Baltimore, 1976), 94.

25 Ibid., 95.

26 Peter De Bolla, *The Discourse of the Sublime: Readings in History, Aesthetics and the Subject* (Oxford, 1989), 44. De Bolla nicely distinguishes between the role of the subject in the eighteenth- and nineteenth-century versions of the sublime, as exemplified by Addison and Coleridge, respectively; see 44–8.

27 Taruskin, "Resisting the Ninth" in *Text and Act* (New York, 1995), 247.

28 Crotch, *Substance of Several Lectures on Music* (London, 1831); excerpted in *Music and Aesthetics in the Eighteenth and Early Nineteenth Centuries*, ed. Peter Le Huray and James Day (Cambridge, 1981), 431.

29 *Berlinische musikalische Zeitung*, vol. I, no. 46; excerpted and trans. in *Music and Aesthetics*, ed. Le Huray and Day, 289–91.

30 Burke, *A Philosophical Enquiry*, part II, section 5, 64.

31 Kant, *Critique of Judgment*, §26, pp. 92 and 90.

32 Franz Schalk, *Briefe und Betrachtungen*, ed. Lili Schalk (Vienna, 1935), 81.

33 Richard Cohn, "Maximally Smooth Cycles, Hexatonic Systems, and the Analysis of Late Romantic Triadic Progressions," *Music Analysis* 15 (1996), 11.

34 Review of a performance of the Adagio of the Seventh Symphony on piano, by Joseph Schalk, Wiener akademischer Wagner-Verein, 4 November 1884, *Neue Zeitschrift für Musik* 80 (1884), 522; quoted in Othmar Wessely, "Bruckner Berichterstattung in der *Neue Zeitschrift für Musik*" in *Bruckner-Symposion: Bruckner Rezeption*, ed. Wessely (Linz, 1991), 140.

35 Robert Simpson mentioned the significance of the voicing of this chord in *The Essence of Bruckner*, rev. edn. (London, 1992), 199.

36 Artur Schopenhauer, *The World as Will and Representation*, trans. E. F. J. Payne, 2 vols. (New York, 1969), §39, vol. I, 202.

37 Kant, *Critique of Judgment*, §26, p. 91.

38 Raimonda Modiano, "Humanism and the Comic Sublime: From Kant to Friedrich Theodor Vischer," *Studies in Romanticism* 26 (1987), 235.

39 Review of Bruckner's Eighth Symphony, *Neue Freie Presse*, 23 December 1892; rpt. in Eduard Hanslick, *Fünf Jahre Musik* (Berlin, 1899), 190–1; English trans. in Eduard Hanslick, *Music Criticisms 1846–99*, trans. Henry Pleasants (Baltimore, 1950), 288–9, translation modified.

40 On Viennese liberalism and music see Leon Botstein, "Time and Memory: Concert Life, Science, and Music in Brahms's Vienna" in *Brahms and His World*, ed. Walter Frisch (Princeton, 1990), 3–22 and Margaret Notley, "Brahms as Liberal: Genre, Style, and Politics in Late Nineteenth-Century Vienna," *19th-Century Music* 17 (1993), 107–23.

41 *Deutsche Zeitung*, 5 November 1896; quoted in Notley, "Brahms as Liberal," 109, translation modified.

42 Felix Wartenegg in *Neue Zeitschrift für Musik* 87 (1891), 80; quoted in Wessely, "Bruckner Berichterstattung in der *Neue Zeitschrift für Musik*," 140.

43 Eduard Hanslick, *On the Musically Beautiful*, trans. Geoffrey Payzant (Indianapolis, 1986), see esp. 28 and 5.

44 See Weber, *The Protestant Ethic and the Spirit of Capitalism*, trans. Talcott Parsons (New York, 1958); also see Herbert Marcuse's critical view in "Industrialization and Capitalism in the Work of Max Weber" in *Negations: Essays in Critical Theory* (Boston, 1968), 201–27.

45 See Marie-Hélène Huet, "The Revolutionary Sublime," *Eighteenth-Century Studies* 28 (1994), 51–64.

46 William R. Musgrave, "'That Monstrous Fiction': Radical Agency and Aesthetic Ideology in Burke," *Studies in Romanticism* 36 (1997), 10.

47 *Wiener Allgemeine Zeitung*, quoted in Max Auer, *Anton Bruckner: Seine Leben und Schaffen* (Vienna, 1947), 381.

48 Max Graf, *The Legend of a Musical City* (New York, 1945), 136.

5 The 1887 version and the 1890 version

1 Robert Haas, "Einführung" in *Anton Bruckner Sämtliche Werke, 8. Band: VIII. Symphonie C-moll (Originalfassung), Studienpartitur*, ed. Haas (Leipzig, 1939).

2 See Max Auer, "Die biographischen Tatsachen" in *Anton Bruckner: wissenschaftliche und künstlerische Betrachtungen zu den Originalfassungen* (Vienna, 1937), 10–11 and Robert Haas, "Vorlagenbericht" in *Anton Bruckner Sämtliche Werke, 4. Band/I. Teil: IV. Symphonie Es-Dur (Fassung von 1878 mit dem Finale von 1880), Finale von 1878, Partituren und Entwürfe mit Bericht*, ed. Haas (Vienna, 1936).

3 Haas, "Einführung" in *VIII. Symphonie C-moll*. Haas followed a rather similar editorial method in his edition of the Second Symphony.

4 Cooke, "Anton Bruckner" in *The New Grove Dictionary of Music and Musicians*, ed. Stanley Sadie (London, 1980), vol. III, 361–2; rpt. in *New Grove Late Romantic Masters* (New York and London, 1985), 34–6; also see his "The Bruckner Problem Simplified" in *Vindications: Essays on Romantic Music* (Cambridge, 1982), 65–9.

5 As Bruckner's friend and student Friedrich Eckstein put it: "I can testify that it was impossible to coerce him in artistic matters"; quoted in "Leidenschaftliche Erörterungen um Bruckner," *Anbruch* 18 (1936), 48. Similar sentiments were offered by Friedrich Klose, response to Alfred Orel's "Original und Bearbeitung bei Anton Bruckner," *Deutsche Musikkultur* 1 (1936/37), 223 and Josef V. von Wöss in comments quoted in Max Morold, "Noch einiges zur Bruckner-Frage," *Zeitschrift für Musik* 103 (1936), 1188.

6 Max Auer, "Der Streit um den 'echten' Bruckner," *Zeitschrift für Musik* 103 (1936), 542.

7 Nowak, "Vorwort" in *Anton Bruckner Sämtliche Werke, Band 8: VIII. Symphonie C-moll, Fassung von 1890*, 2. Revidierte Ausgabe (Vienna, 1955).

8 Quoted in Constantin Floros, "Die Fassungen der Achten Symphonie von Anton Bruckner" in *Bruckner-Symposion: Die Fassungen*, ed. Franz Grasberger (Linz, 1981), 53.

9 Letter of 7 October 1887; see p. 18 above.

10 On the use of Wagner tubas in symphonic music see Stephen Parkany, "Kurth's *Bruckner* and the Adagio of Bruckner's Seventh Symphony," *19th-Century Music* 11 (1988), 269.

11 Bryan Gilliam points out several other subtle motivic links in "The Two Versions of Bruckner's Eighth Symphony," *19th-Century Music* 16 (1992), 62, note 13.

12 Kurth, *Bruckner* (Berlin, 1925), 1077.

13 Bruckner did replace a few pages of the score, but the majority of the cuts were effected by simple crossing out; see Dermot Gault, "For Later Times," *Musical Times* 137 (1996), 17.

14 Letter dated 8 April 1891, now in the Bayerische Staatsbibliothek (Munich), Leviana. I am grateful to Laurence Dreyfus for sharing this letter with me.

15 See Bruckner, *Vorlesungen über Harmonielehre und Kontrapunkt an der Universität Wien*, ed. Ernst Schwanzara (Vienna, 1950), 201–2.

16 See Wagner, *Bruckner: Leben, Werke, Dokumente* (Mainz, 1983), 394–6 and *Der Wandel des Konzepts: zu den verschiedenen Fassungen von Bruckners Dritter, Vierter und Achter Sinfonie* (Vienna, 1980).

17 See Gilliam, "The Two Versions of Bruckner's Eighth Symphony," 62–4, 69.

18 Ibid., 63.

6 The 1892 edition, authorship, and performance practice

1 See Benjamin Korstvedt, "The First Printed Edition of Anton Bruckner's Fourth Symphony: Collaboration and Authenticity," *19th-Century Music* 20 (1996), 3–26 and William Carragan, "Introduction" in *Anton Bruckner Sämtliche Werke, Band 2: II. Symphonie C-moll, Fassung 1887/1892, Studienpartitur* (Vienna, in press).

2 Benjamin Korstvedt, "'Return to the Pure Sources': The Ideology and Text-Critical Legacy of the First Bruckner *Gesamtausgabe*" in *Bruckner Studies*, ed. Timothy Jackson and Paul Hawkshaw (Cambridge, 1997), 91–109.

3 Wills, *John Wayne's America: The Politics of Celebrity* (New York, 1997), 26.

4 Only the Scherzo (copied by Leopold Hofmeyer) is currently preserved, in the Gesellschaft der Musikfreunde in Vienna (A-Wgm XIII 32.394W). In 1994 another late manuscript copy (not an autograph) of the score appeared on the market, and was purchased by a private collector; see Andrea Harrandt, "Unbekannte Bruckner-Autographe entdeckt," *Österreichische Musikzeitschrift* 49 (1994), 32.

5 See Oberleithner, *Meine Erinnerungen an Anton Bruckner* (Regensburg, 1933), 52–3 and Leopold Nowak, "Anton Bruckners Achte Symphonie und ihre zweite Fassung" in *Über Anton Bruckner* (Vienna, 1985), 28.

6 See Robert Haas, "Einführung" in *Anton Bruckner Sämtliche Werke, 8. Band: VIII. Symphonie C-moll (Originalfassung), Studienpartitur*, ed. Haas (Leipzig, 1939).

7 Franz Grasberger, *Anton Bruckner zwischen Wagnis und Sicherheit (eine Ausstellung)* (Linz, 1977), 56 and Thomas Leibnitz, *Die Brüder Schalk und Anton Bruckner* (Tutzing, 1988), 276.

8 Grasberger, *Anton Bruckner zwischen Wagnis und Sicherheit*, 56; Nowak, "Anton Bruckners Achte Symphonie," 28; and Leibnitz, *Die Brüder Schalk und Anton Bruckner*, 276. Emphasis in the original.

9 See for example Paul Hawkshaw, "The Bruckner Problem Revisited,"

19th-Century Music 21 (1997), 100–1, where the source of this quotation is mistakenly given as the letter of 31 July 1891.

10 Although the handwriting is not entirely clear, Schalk almost certainly wrote "gestrichenen," as can be confirmed from the facsimile in Franz Grasberger, *Anton Bruckner zum 150. Geburtstag (eine Ausstellung)* (Vienna, 1974), 33. Note that in 1977 in *Anton Bruckner zwischen Wagnis und Sicherheit* Grasberger did transcribe this word as "gestrichenen."

11 These portions of the letters have been published only in Grasberger, *Anton Bruckner zwischen Wagnis und Sicherheit*, 56. All subsequent quotations are from this source.

12 See Ernst Kurth, *Anton Bruckner* (Berlin, 1925), 1331.

13 Gault, "For Later Times," *Musical Times* 137 (1996), 18. Gault states that the cut covers bars 325–86, but this is undoubtedly a misprint for 345–86.

14 Hawkshaw, "The Bruckner Problem Revisited," 104, where Hawkshaw does make this claim about the Eighth Symphony.

15 See Korstvedt, "The First Printed Edition of Anton Bruckner's Fourth Symphony" and Thomas Röder, *Anton Bruckner Sämtliche Werke, Band 3: III. Symphonie D-moll, Revisionsbericht* (Vienna, 1997), esp. 241–6 and 331–41.

16 See Lili Schalk, "Gespräche über Bruckner mit Franz," unpublished typescript and Wöss, unpublished letter to Wilhelm Furtwängler dated 23 April 1936 (both Wn F 18 Schalk 360/4/3–4). Wöss was proof-reader, and eventually director, of Waldheim-Eberle, the firm that engraved all of Bruckner's editions, including the Eighth Symphony, published after 1890.

17 Wagner, "Bruckners Sinfonie-Fassungen – gründsätzlich referiert" in *Bruckner-Symposion: Die Fassungen*, ed. Franz Grasberger (Linz, 1981), 18.

18 Letter to Nikisch, 5 November 1884, Anton Bruckner, *Gesammelte Briefe*, neue Folge, ed. Max Auer (Regensburg, 1924), 170.

19 Letter to Weingartner, 27 January 1891; *Briefe*, ed. Auer, 237.

20 See Korstvedt, "The First Printed Edition of Anton Bruckner's Fourth Symphony," 13–16.

21 Erich Leinsdorf, *The Composer's Advocate: a Radical Orthodoxy for Musicians* (New Haven, 1981), 198.

22 Letter of 20 March 1891; *Briefe*, ed. Auer, 368.

23 Letter of 27 March 1891; *Briefe*, ed. Auer, 241.

24 The dynamic character of a few passages is altered more fundamentally, notably the addition of a diminuendo to the pealing horns and trumpets in mm. 386–9 of the first movement and the lowering of mm. 301–8 of the Finale from *fortissimo* to something like *mezzo-forte*. Also, a few big tuttis that are presented as a steady *fortissimo* in the 1890 version are made to build

gradually to this peak of loudness in the 1892 edition; e.g., mm. 183–211 and mm. 679–86 of the Finale.

25 Comment dated 20 October 1924 in Schalk, "Gespräche über Bruckner mit Franz."

26 Eugen Jochum, "The Interpretation of Bruckner's Symphonies," essay accompanying *Bruckner: 9 Symphonies*, cond. Eugen Jochum (DGG 429 079–2).

27 For some reason, conductors almost never follow the metronome markings in this movement. As a rule, the opening tempo is taken more quickly than indicated and the second significantly more slowly; yet this is probably exactly what Bruckner's metronome markings were designed to avoid!

28 Floros, "Historische Phasen der Bruckner-Interpretation" in *Bruckner-Symposion: Bruckner-Interpretation*, ed. Frans Grasberger (Linz, 1982), 99. For another important discussion of tempo schemes, see William Carragan, "Reconstructing Bruckner's Tempos," *American Record Guide*, Nov./Dec. 1996, 73–5 and 177.

29 Philip, "Flexibility of Tempo" in *Early Recordings and Musical Style: Changing Tastes in Instrumental Performance, 1900–1950* (Cambridge, 1992), 7–36, also 38–41.

30 Wagner, *Über das Dirigieren*, trans. Eduard Dannreuther as *On Conducting* (London, 1887; rpt. New York, 1989), 92–3, also 43 and 67.

31 Franz Schalk, *Briefe und Betrachtungen*, ed. Lili Schalk (Vienna, 1935), 83–4.

32 Discographic details for Table 6.3: Walter, New York Philharmonic, concert performance, 26 January 1941 (Historical Performers 23); Karajan, Preussische Staatskapelle, radio broadcast, September 1944 (Koch/Schwann 314482); Furtwängler, Vienna Philharmonic, concert performance, 17 October 1944 (Unicorn 109–10); Furtwängler, Berlin Philharmonic, concert performance, 14 March 1949 (EMI 5 66210 2); Jochum, Hamburg State Philharmonic, 1949 (DG 449 758–2); Knappertsbusch, Berlin Philharmonic, concert performance, 7–8 January 1951 (Music and Arts 856); Furtwängler, Vienna Philharmonic, concert performance, 10 April 1954 (Fonit Cetra FE 17); Schuricht, Vienna Philharmonic, 1964 (EMI CZS7 67279–2); Jochum, Berlin Philharmonic, 1964 (DG 429 079–2); Böhm, Vienna Philharmonic, 1977 (DG 2709 068); Masur, Gewandhaus Orchestra Leipzig, June 1978 (Eurodisc 300 639–440); Barenboim, Chicago Symphony Orchestra, 1981 (DG 2740 253); Giulini, Vienna Philharmonic, 1984 (DG 415 124–1); Karajan, Vienna Philharmonic, 1988 (DG 427 611–2); Maazel, Berlin Philharmonic, 1990 (EMI 69796–2); Eichhorn, Bruckner Orchestra Linz, July 1991 (Camerata 225); Lopez-Cobos, Cincinnati Symphony Orchestra, 14–15 March 1993 (Telarc 80343); Wand, North German

Radio Symphony Orchestra, 5–7 December 1993, concert performance (RCA 68047–2); Dohnanyi, Cleveland Orchestra, 6–7 February 1994 (London 443 753–2).

33 On this issue see Richard Taruskin's thought-provoking meditations in "On Letting the Music Speak for Itself" and "The Pastness of the Present and the Presence of the Past" in *Text and Act* (Oxford, 1995), 51–66, esp. 53–6, and 90–155, esp. 90–102.

34 Wilhelm Furtwängler, "Anton Bruckner: Vortrag gehalten anläßlich des 1. Großdeutschen Brucknerfestes in Wien (1939)" quoted in Keith Cunliffe, "Furtwängler and Bruckner," *Newsletter of the Wilhelm Furtwängler Society, UK* 95 (April and June, 1989), n.p.

35 Simpson, *The Essence of Bruckner*, rev. edn. (London, 1992), 231.

Appendix A

1 Haas, "Einführung" in *Anton Bruckner Sämtliche Werke, 8. Band: VIII. Symphonie C-moll (Originalfassung), Studienpartitur*, ed. Haas (Leipzig, 1939).

2 See Leopold Nowak, "Anton Bruckners Achte Symphonie und ihre zweite Fassung," *Über Anton Bruckner* (Vienna, 1985), 28.

3 It is interesting to note that Haas did not reintroduce all of the material Bruckner crossed out in his revised score; see Dermot Gault, "For Later Times," *Musical Times* 137 (1996), 17.

4 Quoted in Morten Solvik, "The International Bruckner Society and the N.S.D.A.P.: A Case Study of Robert Haas and the Critical Edition," *Musical Quarterly* 83 (1998), 367. On the ideology of Haas's Bruckner editions also see Benjamin Korstvedt, "'Return to the Pure Sources': The Ideology and Text-Critical Legacy of the First Bruckner *Gesamtausgabe*" in *Bruckner Studies*, ed. Timothy Jackson and Paul Hawkshaw (Cambridge, 1997), 91–109. On Haas's early membership in the Nazi Party and its political advantage after the *Anschluß* see Pamela Maxine Potter, *Most German of the Arts: Musicology and Society from the Weimar Republic to the End of Hitler's Reich* (New Haven, 1998), 115–17.

5 In the United States a photo-reprint of Haas's edition is available from Kalmus (number K 00382).

Appendix B

1 Cooke, "Anton Bruckner" in *The New Grove Dictionary of Music and Musicians*, ed. Stanley Sadie (London, 1980), vol. III, 362; rpt. in *The New Grove Late Romantic Masters* (New York and London, 1985), 36.

Select bibliography

Anton Bruckner: Ein Handbuch, ed. Uwe Harten (Salzburg and Vienna, 1996)

Auer, Max. *Anton Bruckner: Sein Leben und Werk* (Vienna, 1947)

Benjamin, William. "Tonal Dualism in Bruckner's Eighth Symphony" in *The Second Practice of Nineteenth-Century Tonality*, ed. William Kinderman and Harald Krebs (Lincoln, Nebr., 1996), 237–58

Bloch, Ernst. *Essays in the Philosophy of Music*, trans. Peter Palmer (Cambridge, 1985)

Botstein, Leon. "Time and Memory: Concert Life, Science, and Music in Brahms's Vienna" in *Brahms and His World*, ed. Walter Frisch (Princeton, 1990), 3–22

Brinkmann, Reinhold. *Late Idyll: The Second Symphony of Johannes Brahms*, trans. Peter Palmer (Cambridge, Mass., 1995)

Bruckner, Anton. *Gesammelte Briefe*, ed. Franz Gräflinger (Regensburg, 1924)

Gesammelte Briefe, neue Folge, ed. Max Auer (Regensburg, 1924)

Carragan, William. "Reconstructing Bruckner's Tempos," *American Record Guide*, Nov./Dec. 1996, 73–5 and 177

Cooke, Deryck. "Anton Bruckner" in *The New Grove Dictionary of Music and Musicians*, ed. Stanley Sadie (London, 1980), vol. III, 352–71; rpt. in *The New Grove Late Romantic Masters* (London, 1985), 1–73

"The Bruckner Problem Simplified" in *Vindications: Essays on Romantic Music* (Cambridge, 1982), 43–71

Dahlhaus, Carl. "Issues in Composition" in *Between Romanticism and Modernism*, trans. Mary Whittall (Berkeley and Los Angeles, 1980), 40–78

"Bruckner und die Programmusik: zum Finale der Achten Symphonie" in *Anton Bruckner: Studien zu Werk und Wirkung, Walter Wiora zum 30. Dezember 1986* (Tutzing, 1988), 7–32

The Idea of Absolute Music, trans. Roger Lustig (Chicago, 1989)

Dawson-Bowling, Paul. "Thematic and Tonal Unity in Bruckner's Eighth Symphony," *Music Review* 30 (1969), 225–36

Doernberg, Erwin. *The Life and Symphonies of Anton Bruckner* (London, 1960)

Floros, Constantin. *Brahms und Bruckner: Studien zur Musikalischen Exegetik* (Wiesbaden, 1980)

"Die Fassungen der Achten Symphonie von Anton Bruckner" in *Bruckner-Symposion: Die Fassungen*, ed. Franz Grasberger (Linz, 1981), 53–63

"Historische Phasen der Bruckner-Interpretation" in *Bruckner-Symposion*: *Bruckner-Interpretation*, ed. Franz Grasberger (Linz, 1982), 93–102

Gault, Dermot. "For Later Times," *Musical Times* 137 (1996), 12–19

Gilliam, Bryan. "The Two Versions of Bruckner's Eighth Symphony," *19th-Century Music* 16 (1992), 59–69

Göllerich, August and Max Auer. *Anton Bruckner: Ein Lebens- und Schaffensbild*, 4 vols. in 9 parts (Regensburg, 1922–37)

Gräflinger, Franz. *Anton Bruckner: Leben und Schaffen (Umgearbeitete Bausteine)* (Berlin, 1927)

Grasberger, Franz. *Anton Bruckner zum 150. Geburtstag (eine Ausstellung)* (Vienna, 1974)

Anton Bruckner zwischen Wagnis und Sicherheit (eine Ausstellung) (Linz, 1977)

"Das Bruckner-Bild der Zeitung 'Das Vaterland' in den Jahren 1870–1900" in *Festschrift Hans Schneider zum 60. Geburtstag*, ed. Rudolf Elvers and Ernst Vogel (Munich, 1981), 113–32

Grunsky, Karl. *Anton Bruckner* (Stuttgart, 1922)

Haas, Frithjof. *Zwischen Brahms und Wagner: Der Dirigent Hermann Levi* (Zurich, 1995)

Haas, Robert. *Anton Bruckner* (Potsdam, 1934)

Hanslick, Eduard. *Music Criticisms 1846–99*, trans. Henry Pleasants (Baltimore, 1950)

On the Musically Beautiful, trans. Geoffrey Payzant (Indianapolis, 1986)

Horn, Erwin. "Evolution und Metamorphose in der Achten Symphonie von Anton Bruckner: Darstellung der thematischen Zusammenhänge," *Bruckner Jahrbuch 1989/90* (Linz, 1992), 7–34

Johnson, Stephen, ed. *Bruckner Remembered* (London, 1998)

Kähler, Willibald. "Sinfonie No. VIII (C moll)" in *Bruckner's Symphonien*, Meisterführer Nr. 4, ed. Karl Grunsky (Berlin and Vienna, n.d. [1907]), 152–69

Korstvedt, Benjamin. "Anton Bruckner in the Third Reich and After: An Essay on Ideology and Bruckner Reception," *Musical Quarterly* 80 (1996), 132–60

"'Return to the Pure Sources': The Ideology and Text-Critical Legacy of the First Bruckner *Gesamtausgabe*" in *Bruckner Studies*, ed. Timothy Jackson and Paul Hawkshaw (Cambridge, 1997), 91–109

Korte, Werner. *Bruckner und Brahms: die spätromantische Lösung der autonomen Konzeption* (Tutzing, 1963)

Kurth, Ernst. *Anton Bruckner* (Berlin, 1925)

Leibnitz, Thomas. *Die Brüder Schalk und Anton Bruckner* (Tutzing, 1988)

Leichtentritt, Hugo. "Anton Bruckner: The Eighth Symphony" in *Musical Form* (Cambridge, Mass., 1961), 379–424

Nägler, Norbert. "Bruckners gründerzeitliche Monumentalsymphonie," *Musik-Konzepte 23/24: Anton Bruckner* (Munich, 1982), 86–118

Notley, Margaret. "Brahms as Liberal: Genre, Style, and Politics in Late Nineteenth-Century Vienna," *19th-Century Music* 17 (1993), 107–23

"*Volksconcerte* in Vienna and Late-Nineteenth Century Ideology of the Symphony," *Journal of the American Musicological Society* 50 (1997), 421–53

Nowak, Leopold. "Die Anton Bruckner-Gesamtausgabe: Ihre Geschichte und Schicksale," *Bruckner Jahrbuch 1982/83* (Linz, 1984), 33–67

"Anton Bruckners Achte Symphonie und ihre zweite Fassung" in *Über Anton Bruckner* (Vienna, 1985), 27–9

Oberleithner, Max von. *Meine Erinnerungen an Anton Bruckner* (Regensburg, 1933)

Orel, Alfred. *Anton Bruckner: Das Werk, der Künstler, die Zeit* (Vienna, 1925)

Parkany, Stephen. "Kurth's *Bruckner* and the Adagio of the Seventh Symphony," *19th-Century Music* 9 (1988), 262–81

Röthig, Claudia. *Studien zur Systematik des Schaffens von Anton Bruckner* (Göttingen, 1978)

Schalk, Franz. *Briefe und Betrachtungen*, ed. Lili Schalk (Vienna, 1935)

Schenker, Heinrich. *Heinrich Schenker als Essayist und Kritiker: gesammelte Aufsätze, Rezensionen und kleinere Berichte aus den Jahren 1891–1901*, ed. Hellmut Federhofer (Hildesheim, 1990)

Scott, Derek. "Bruckner and the Dialectic of Darkness and Light," *Bruckner Journal* 2/1 (1998), 12–14; 2/2 (1998), 12–14; 3/1 (1998), 13–15; 3/2 (forthcoming)

Simpson, Robert. *The Essence of Bruckner*, rev. edn. (London, 1992)

Sisman, Elaine. *Mozart: The Jupiter Symphony*, Cambridge Music Handbooks (Cambridge, 1993)

Taruskin, Richard. *Text and Act* (Oxford, 1995)

Wagner, Manfred. *Der Wandel des Konzepts: zu den verschiedenen Fassungen von Bruckners Dritter, Vierter und Achter Sinfonie* (Vienna, 1980)

Bruckner: Leben, Werke, Dokumente (Mainz, 1983)

"Zur Rezeptionsgeschichte von Anton Bruckners Achter Symphonie," *Bruckner Jahrbuch 1991/92/93* (Linz, 1995), 109–15

Weiskel, Thomas. *The Romantic Sublime: Studies in the Structure and Psychology of Transcendence* (Baltimore, 1976)

Index